MW00736858

FROM A CHINESE CITY

BY GONTRAN DE PONCINS

FROM A CHINESE CITY

GONTRAN DE PONCINS

Translated from the French by
BERNARD FRECHTMAN

Introduction by
EDWARD L. ROBINSON

TRACKLESS SANDS PRESS
PALO ALTO

Copyright © 1957 by Gontran de Poncins. First published in 1957 by
Doubleday and Company. This edition published in 1991 by arrangement
with Doubleday, a division of Bantam Doubleday Dell Publishing Group, Inc.
Introduction copyright © 1991 by Trackless Sands Press.

Published in the United States by
Trackless Sands Press
Palo Alto, California

All rights reserved, including, without limitation, the right of the publisher to
sell directly to end users of this and other Trackless Sands Press books. No
part of this book may be reproduced in any form or by any electronic or
mechanical means, including information storage and retrieval systems,
without permission in writing from the publisher, except by a reviewer who
may quote brief passages in a review.

Trackless Sands Press and its colophon are registered trademarks
of Glasford Brothers, Incorporated

Printed on acid-free paper
Manufactured in the United States of America

The paper used in this publication meets the requirements
for permanence established by the American National Standard
for Information Sciences–Permanence of Paper for Printed
Library Materials, ANSI 439.48.1984

Library of Congress Cataloging-in-Publication Data

Poncins, Gontran de Montaigne, vicomte de, 1900–1962
        [D'une ville chinoise. English]
        From a Chinese City / by Gontran de Poncins; translated by
Bernard Frechtman.
                        p.   cm.
        Translation of: D'une ville chinoise.
        Reprint. Originally published: Garden City, N.Y.: Doubleday &
Co., 1957.
        ISBN 1-879434-01-6 : $19.95 — ISBN 1-879434-00-8 (pbk.):
$11.95
        1. Chinese in Vietnam. 2. Cho Lon, Vietnam—Social Life and
Customs.
DS557.A5P673 1991
915.97—dc20   91-065340
                                                            CIP

INTRODUCTION

Edward L. Robinson

MONSIEUR Gontran de Poncins, a solitary traveler recording with pen and brush the genius of cultures hidden away in remote corners of the world, wrote this journal in his walk-up room in the Sun Wah Hotel in Cholon. He chose Cholon, the Chinese riverbank community snuggled up to Saigon, because he suspected that the ancient customs of a national culture endure longer in remote colonies than in the motherland. In effect, he was studying a bit of ancient China, untouched at the time—this was 1955—by the Communist government. The Cholon he visited was a most insular city-within-a city, some six hundred and fifty thousand Chinese busily carrying on their commerce and industry in concert with the Vietnamese.

Anyone who stays for any time in the cities of Southeast Asia comes to realize that the energetic and frugal Chinese tend to monopolize the local world of trade. They do this, as a rule, rather unostentatiously, though the more affluent do occasionally erect grand residential manors. It was not the giants of commerce who interested de Poncins; he was interested primarily in the common folk, the mix of people

I

who provide the color of street life in Asia. de Poncins dug into the right place. Cholon was a teeming, swarming beehive of activity that seldom paused day or night.

"Go to Cholon," the author's guide and mentor suggested when he landed at the Saigon dock. "Cholon is China. Go find life in a Chinese hotel." And what was unique about Cholon? Cholon "ignores the West," the author's guide replied, "and has no desire to mingle with it, except in night clubs—though even there the contact is only apparent and the dangers of contamination are reduced to a minimum. Cholon will teach you a great deal, if it is the Chinese mind and Chinese life you are interested in. But you'll have to rid yourself, as far as possible, of your Western concept."

Acting on his guide's advice, the author courageously planted himself in the modest Sun Wah Hotel, smack on Cholon's main street. There he became an object of great curiosity for the Chinese, who politely monitored his every move, frequently peering into his room, as it was deemed impolite to close the door.

So began his education. In short order he found himself embroiled in his adopted community, venturing forth each day to study life about him. His search for the essence of Chinese motivation and behavior is the heart of this story. Everything he saw intrigued him—Chinese eating habits, their work ethics, their medical practices, their elaborate theater, their aesthetic talents, their varied physiognomies, their rich philosophy—indeed, everything. All this is laid out for the reader, written with a light and humorous hand, just as it was lived by the author. As a writer and as an artist, de Poncins also shows us the beauty in commonplace things: the street vendor's display of lettuce; the water-lily leaf folded into a sack to carry a live fish; the artistry of motion of the sampans on the river, poled by bent figures with supple reeds.

The author visited Cholon at a time when the French had admitted defeat in their long struggle with the Viet-namese and the United States had not yet become bogged down in its own misadventures in Vietnam. Neither the French nor the North American troubles intrude on this story. War is mercifully absent until the very end.

I happened to live in Saigon thirty years ago, shortly after de Poncins made his visit. The members of the American mission at the time were consumed, of course, with politics. However, politics in Vietnam grew out of the desires and needs of people driven by cultural forces we never under-stood. This is a subject too burdensome and complex to go into here, but it is no secret that we were operating in an area where the local citizens, both Chinese and Vietnamese, simply bewildered us. We did not understand the bitter animosity on the part of the Vietnamese toward China, still seen as an ancient adversary, a foe that conquered and occupied Vietnam for an entire millennium. Yet in spite of the animosity between the nations, Chinese Confucian influence runs deep into the fabric of Vietnamese society. The cultures are intertwined. Thus, in this book we can learn a good bit about the Vietnamese as well as the expa-triate Chinese.

The final chapter of the book describes the turbulence overwhelming Cholon in the spring of 1955, when the government of President Ngo Dinh Diem attacked the notorious piratical band known as the Binh-Xuyen. South Vietnam had more than its share of bizarre political-religious sects, the most durable being the Hoa-Hao and the Cao-

3

Dai. Most survived the tumult of war, though the Binh-Xuyen were finally put out of commission on the outskirts of Saigon and flushed into the swamps. But not before they had caused vast destruction, as de Poncins describes.

The Binh-Xuyen had hooked up with the Cao-Dai and the Hoa-Hao to form a common front. In January of 1955, President Diem shut down the Binh-Xuyen gambling casinos in one of his outbursts of puritanical reform. By the end of March, fighting started in Saigon and spread to Cholon. The North Americans on the scene at first leaned toward supporting the pirates in hopes of dumping Diem, but as so often happened, events forced them to switch sides. The whole affair was filled with intrigue. The most colorful North American on hand was Colonel Edward G. Lansdale, who befriended Diem and reportedly thereby became the prototype for the main character in *The Quiet American,* Graham Greene's incisive novel. The battle with the Binh-Xuyen could have gone either way. President Diem could have been toppled and history would have been different, though my hunch is it would have been just as disastrous.

de Poncins displayed remarkable clairvoyance. He wrote, "The upheaval in Indo-China had only just begun. The French, who had been kept there by business, were beginning to leave the country. When they were gone there would be a vacuum, a vacuum that would not be filled by Mr. Diem's Vietnamese, who were quite incapable of filling it. It would be filled by the Viets of the North, the Communists, and also, no doubt, in the commercial sphere, by the Japanese . . ."

At the time, a mere handful of North American officials viewed the situation in the same way, and they were quickly discredited by higher authority. It is most interesting that this lone Frenchman, a newcomer, could absorb enough feeling for the realities of life to see that the emperor wore no clothes, as it were. President Diem was a Catholic autocrat from the North who never would capture the allegiance of the common people and who finally paid a fearful price for his shaky performance.

Few of the subsequent leaders of South Vietnam were appreciably more successful, and some were undoubtedly more corrupt. We, the citizens of the United States, were hornswoggled by so many tinhorn politicians and generals that we lost our sense of reality. Indeed, our last ambassador was busily enticing North American businessmen to invest in Vietnam even as indomitable armies of the North were moving in to crush Saigon.

At the close of the book, the author conjectures that following the 1955 fighting the Chinese of Cholon would have to seek a new place to live. But evidence we have now suggests this did not happen on a large scale. The Chinese dug in and hung on, although following the triumph of the Communists in 1975, the Chinese were periodically harassed by the new government. In the late 1970s, the government attempted to take over the activities of the Chinese businessmen who dominated trade, particularly the vital rice trade. However, as generally happened under Communist rule, the new system didn't work, and gradually the Chinese regained their influence. Then came the border skirmishes between Vietnam and China, which so alarmed the Vietnamese government that they forced many thousands of Chinese to leave the country. Many were trucked to the border and summarily dumped. They remain in China today, in villages along the border. Despite those deportations and other persecutions, the Chinese citizenry of Cholon remained largely intact and no doubt is playing a significant role in the slow economic revival of Vietnam.

Who was this curious man who wrote such an insightful book? His full name was Vicomte Gontran Jean-Pierre de Montaigne de Poncins, a direct descendant of the most widely read writer of the French Renaissance, Michel de Montaigne. Although de Poncins never mentions his lineage in the book, he too was a true Renaissance man: He was soldier, linguist, business executive, reporter, parachutist, anthropologist, moralist, and painter. He was born 19 August 1900, on his family's nine-hundred-year-old estate in southeast France. Educated by clerics on the family estate until age fourteen, he followed the usual aristocratic path to military school and, finally, Saint Cyr, the French equivalent of West Point. World War I ended before he could enter the conflict, so he joined the army as a private (scandalizing his family, his widow reveals) and served with the French mission assigned to the American Army of Occupation in Germany. He learned English and subsequently numerous other languages. He became interested in human psychology, searching, he said, for what it is that helps people make their way through life. He joined the Paris École des Beaux-Arts and painted there for six years, then entered an Italian silk concern and rose to become its manager in London. But something in the business world disenchanted him, and he left to travel, restlessly, through India and China and the South Seas, writing of his experiences for newspapers and magazines.

While a writer in the United States in 1938, he arranged to visit the Eskimo. He made his way to Canada's King

6

William Island, north of the Arctic Circle, where he settled down to live among the Netsilik Eskimo. This adventure produced his first book, *Kabloona*, named after an Eskimo word for *outsider*. It became a selection of the Book-of-the-Month Club, sold two million copies in the early forties, and brought him fame. In *Kabloona*, he wrote, "Hardest of all was not the severity of the climate, not the intensity of the cold, nor the physical anguish which, often, I endured. The cold was a problem, but a very much more difficult problem was the Eskimo mentality. There is no getting on with the Eskimo except on his terms, and I had to get on with him if I was to live with him. A good part of this book, therefore, is the story of the encounter of two mentalities, and of the gradual substitution of the Eskimo mentality within myself." In a 1990 *Washington Post Book World* note, George Simeon, a later-day *kabloona*, touted his rediscovery of this "work of timeless value," describing the charm of all de Poncin's writing: The reader experiences the feeling of kinship with another society.

Madame Therizol de Poncins, the author's widow, wrote in October 1990 to the editor of this edition, "It will be difficult to express in a few sentences the essentials of a life that was full of sentiment, suffering, and reversals yet rich in action, and rich, as well, in a search for inner peace. My husband's early life was comfortable, opulent, and pleasurable. Yet he was given a strict moral upbringing by a private religious tutor, who, among others, taught him the principles that were such a part of the aristocracy. Hence, his sense of honor and, I suggest, his introspection. He sought the unity and simplicity of what is essential. He died having had the courage to intensely live life, accepting its joys and hardships as signposts toward fulfillment and destiny.

7

"After World War II, finding his baronial estate looted, he wanted to start again, someplace far away. He sought out some of the famous lone explorers and visionaries of his day, including Teilhard de Chardin in China. It was after his last trip to China that he met up with his parents again. They were soon to die in their castle. He agreed to part with the family's nine-hundred-year-old estate, in a financial arrangement that turned sour. He turned his back on the old aristocracy and on his childhood friends, who were obsessed with deer-stalking and duck-shooting parties.

"It was during this period in his life that we met and were married. I encouraged him to think about what was truly important in his life: what he had learned in travel, his hardships, his self-discovery. He started to look for a place where he could spend his last years—he had become ill. Quite by chance, he found a small estate in our luminous Provence, a southeast part of France where I am from, in a magical scenic spot: the kind of place he could best assess his life's journey. He tried to say, in his last book, *Le Matin de L'Homme*, published six months after his death, that rather than living in the "illusionary cone," you can find, in nature, in the stillness of this bounteous country, some of the answers to a lifelong search. It must have been his most significant expedition."

Edward L. Robinson is an "old Asia hand." Author of the novel Sloth and Heathen Folly, *he is a former career foreign service officer with postings in Burma, Vietnam, India, and Germany.*

FOREWORD

THE reader will probably be surprised to note that my account of Chinese life is set in a city that is not in China proper. I should like to explain this seeming anomaly. Though Cholon—or T'ai Ngon, as the Chinese call it—is at present part of Vietnam, it is nonetheless Chinese. While the China of Mao Tse-tung is being radically transformed, Cholon has retained the spirit and traditional forms of ancient China. One of the curious phenomena of the modern world is the fact that local color and old customs are beginning to disappear in certain countries, though they survive intact in a "colony," often a remote one, which, whether out of nostalgia or deep-rooted fidelity to the mother country, has stubbornly conserved them. And so for Cholon. Cholon is one of those cultural islands which, despite the changes that have taken place all about them, have maintained their old ways wonderfully intact. The Chinese community that founded it almost two hundred years ago has retired within itself and, except for business dealings, is utterly indifferent to the rest of the world, to such a de-

9

gree that not once during my entire stay did I hear anyone inquire about what was going on elsewhere. It is this
phenomenon that explains my special interest in observing the community's way of life.

Now that the old forms of Chinese culture and civil-
ization are disappearing, perhaps forever, it seems to me
interesting to cast a last long look at them.

Cholon
February-June, 1955

I

At last I found myself aboard the steamer that was to take me to the Orient. The mooring rope was cast off. I had been beside myself with impatience waiting for this moment to come, for whenever I set foot on a ship I experience a sense of liberation that no land, however far away, can give me. On land I feel myself a prisoner. I am the slave of the contingencies, the absurd constraints, of the modern world. But just give me a boat—any boat —and I'm a free man again!

I had planned to take a cargo boat—for the true-blue traveler, cargo boats are at present the *ne plus ultra* of a sea voyage—a Swedish boat, one of the most luxurious of its kind, which was to take me to Saigon in forty-two days, with stops just about everywhere, and precious ones too, such as those along the Gulf of Persia. It was an ideal plan, for the longer a voyage lasts the better I like it. I have no desire to hurry. Life is too fine an adventure, at least for me, to be scamped.

But my preparations had delayed me longer than they should have, and I was obliged to fall back on the following boat, a man-of-war that was to cover the distance in only eighteen days, with stops at Djibouti, Colombo, and Singapore. That was not too bad either.

But what changes have taken place everywhere since my last visit in 1935! At Djibouti, on the site of the old fort that had dominated the harbor, there was now a spanking-new dock, and huge hangars and oil tanks where once the rocks had sheltered only octopus nests. Djibouti has become the second most important port in the French Union. The result of that development was an odd contrast of berthed liners and Somali *boutres,* of elegant taxis imperiously tooting their horns and small gray donkeys weighed down with their burdens, of oil tanks gleaming in the sun and heaps of old tires and scrap iron—along with the little old-fashioned locomotive, an object out of a Walt Disney film, bristling with beturbaned natives, that wormed its way through the tangle of the port to the accompaniment of its shrill whistle.

Djibouti now has a residential quarter with handsome air-conditioned villas, each with its garden. But Menelick Square is still there with its Bar of the Zinc Palm Tree. The native market has retained its color, and the red-light district, with its soapbox and old board huts, is as dusty as ever. (No doubt the Tourists' Information Bureau has deemed it wise not to tamper with these things.) The women have the same sculptural majesty as in the old days and still smear their faces with saffron to arouse the tourist. Thank God, the picturesque is not yet dead! And the modernization, which has merely been superimposed on the old customs without supplanting them, adds a contrast of its own.

Whenever a transport ship comes alongside, full of sharpshooters back from Indo-China, in no time a traffic is organized, exactly as in the past, with strings and baskets shooting up and down at top speed. Below, the air is filled with shouts and cries, while up above, five hundred heads bending over the toprails lust after the merchandise spread out on the dock: cartons of cigarettes, gleaming rugs, multicolored metal chests. This goes on far into the night. When it is over, the exhausted hawkers fall asleep then and there among their remaining stock.

Sea traffic is certainly increasing everywhere. There was an actual bottleneck at Colombo. Never had I seen such a swarm of men and boats.

There in the silken morning mist more than fifty ships were lined up, the nose of one attached by a buoy to the tail of the other (like elephants moving in single file, each holding by its trunk the tail of the one in front). At nightfall the scene took on a kind of enchantment. The port was like a huge jewel, set with rubies and emeralds. . . .

Ports have a magic all their own, and even the seasoned voyager cannot resist their bewitchment. You rise up from the pit of solitude into which the sea has cast you, and suddenly, in your half-conscious state—for the night was sultry and you yourself weary—you sense a great rumble, followed by the moaning of sirens and the noise of running aboard ship. You leap from your berth and go on deck. All about are ships, more of them than

13

your eyes can take in: destroyers side by side in pairs, sleek as swordfish; triple-decked ocean liners exhaling heavy smoke, sweating water from their portholes; and cargo boats, oozing oil, battered by the sea, but nevertheless doing their job, which is to carry wood, copra, and spices. They are all so crowded together, their ropes and moorings so entangled, that it looks as if a giant spider has woven its web across the port. The air is filled with whistling and hooting and belching of smoke. A thousand launches shoot forward, colliding, tacking about, parting with a spurt of foam. And tenders, too, cling to the flanks of the ships like barnacles. The derricks dart like the antennae of insects; the pulleys creak; and a thousand bales sway in the air.

And then you yourself get caught up in the frenzy. If only you had a dozen pairs of eyes and ears to take it all in! You want to do ten things at once. Everything calls out to you, demands your attention. In a moment you'll be going ashore. And the port will be yours, all yours! Down below, life is awaiting you. For a few Singhalese rupees, a few Hong Kong or Singapore dollars, you will be king! And all things will offer themselves without your even looking for them. The entire town will be open to your desires, and your desires are innumerable. A thousand burning eyes will peer into yours, a thousand hands will reach out to you, eager for your money. And you will be tempted by everything. Every merchant will lay out for you, with a shady gesture of complicity, his tinsel, which will be gold to your bedazzled eyes. Every rickshaw boy will offer to drive you ("You'll give whatever you like, sahib!"). Every wench will be a slave, ready to offer herself, every alley a pathway to adventure. King though you are, it is in vain that you brush aside the crowd with a gesture of contempt; the crowd follows you, presses in on you. And there are the blind old men, each led by a little boy who puts his hand to his mouth in the traditional gesture of hunger; the ragged children swoop down on you like an army of starlings, until they are scattered by the policeman's club. Whereupon there is a vacuum, but only for a moment, for the Orient is a tide that can be pushed back but not contained for long. Typhus, cholera, and leprosy may kill off human beings, but there are always more. Here a man's life has no more weight than a grain of sand. But to your eyes the port is a land of magic, at least during the short time you have had to sample it, for you must be going again.

Wherever I go, in whatever country it may be, I always find someone who has been providentially posted to welcome me. Long ago, in India, my guide and mentor had been so odd-looking a creature that he seemed like a character out of a storybook. He was a puffy-cheeked, merry-eyed professor, with a stray lock of hair like a newborn babe; a great Hindu scholar and learned archaeologist who lived half naked in a dilapidated house, through the openings of which his banana trees were working their way. His only assistant was a native named "Mr. Patabiramain," who doubled as secretary and major-domo. Scholar though he was—he claimed to have an "encyclopedic ignorance"—he bore his learning lightly and had the jollity of an epicurean and the impishness of a child. He was so prankish that he would send me, by special messenger, several rolls of papyrus—in the form of toilet paper—containing thirty yards of a quite unprintable text written out in a broad scrawl. And he also painted for me a picture of India with the clarity and simplicity that are the mark of a superior mind.

Another rare creature, though of a different sort, was waiting for me at the dock in Saigon. All I knew of him was what I had gathered from a hasty exchange of letters before my departure. But I recognized him as soon as I caught sight of him. He was a half-formal-, half-comic-looking character with a stiff collar that went up to his ears, a bald and shiny head, and a mane of long stiff hair that trailed at the back of his neck. He was shortwinded, and his eyes shone with fever. He had, he told me, lost a lung and was on the way to losing the other, though he seemed to be only the more energetic for this. Watching him made me wonder whether the toughest persons aren't those who have been given up by doctors! My new-found friend, a foreigner who had become a French citizen and was consequently all the more French, and even perkier than a Parisian urchin, was a born battler who never ceased fighting with pen and tongue. He was not only a humanist and philosopher, passionately devoted to Mahayana and Zen Buddhism, and editing three reviews, but also a fiery agitator, ready to pour forth to anyone lending an ear. All day long he worked away in a littered den, with his body in a fever and not a penny to his name. But there was no downing him. Though the regime had him ticketed as Enemy Number 1, he nevertheless continued his bitterly sarcastic denunciations of political crimes and scandals. He was, at bottom, a tenderhearted man, given to bursts of violence that were due partly to his state of health, partly to his character. "My house is yours," he said to me with the politeness one acquires in the Orient. "Consider yourself at home!"

Barely had I gone through customs when I felt that shock of the East that runs through me each time I return. It is the swarming of the streets. It is the river with its sampans and miasmas, its vultures describing their stately orbits. It is the streetwalkers with their loose-limbed sway and the loud clacking of their wooden-soled sandals. And more than anything else (for is it not by such things that a country insinuates itself most easily into one's body?) the odor of sizzling fat and spices, the clang-clang of the rickshaws, the cries of the strolling vendors, the provocative laughter of the women.

But, as I promptly discovered, Saigon had changed from what it had been twenty years before. Native handicrafts had been replaced by foreign goods. There, as elsewhere, progress was merely breaking up the old forms, creating a vacuum in which human beings, no longer sheltered within the traditional framework, were at the mercy of the primitive scourges of mankind: hunger, insecurity, fear.

My mentor himself said to me: "Saigon is not the place for you. Clear out of here! Go to Cholon. Cholon is China. Take advantage of the fact that Cholon still exists with its traditional framework and old formulas. Go live in a Chinese hotel. I'll get in touch with some friends and have them find you a room."

The following day I headed for Cholon, escorted by a Chinese. Once again fate was leading me toward the unknown.

II

CHOLON, four miles from Saigon, to which it is linked by a broad, bleak "boulevard," is the Chinese pleasure city. At the "Jade Palace" and "Rainbow" the white man hankering for orientalism fumbles with his chopsticks in an effort to come to grips with the strange foods set before him, and between courses freshens his face with the hot, perfumed napkin handed to him by a Chinese girl whose immobile mask kindles his curiosity and desire.

Cholon is the night city, with electric signs in Chinese characters that gleam like rubies and taxi girls whose shapely bodies stir the customer, who will go off empty-handed, though the attraction retains its compelling force. Cholon is the gambling city; its den, the Wide World, is as famous in its way as the Sex Store of Kobe. Cholon is also the city of opium dives where, for a few piastres, you can have a flap-board bed, a nugget of opium, a boy to prepare your pipes, and, if you so wish, a companion to lie beside you. Cholon is open to all desires. In the eyes of the Chinese, any human desire is legitimate by virtue of its mere existence; in addition, it is a source of profit which he is ever ready to exploit. For anyone touching at Saigon, whether sailor on a spree or tourist eager for the exotic, Cholon is so naturally the pole of attraction that there is no need to tell the rickshaw boy where you want to go. He will take you there straightaway.

But Cholon is something else as well. "Live there," my guide had advised me. "You won't regret it. As time goes by you'll come to know what few Europeans ever do: a Chinese population intensely devoted to its traditions and rites, a city of merchants, with all the pride and standoffishness that the term implies; a society that does not evolve, that refuses to evolve.

"Have you seen Hong Kong? Hong Kong is Chinese but above all it's international. It straddles two cultures, owing to its peculiar status, which makes the Chinese living there citizens of Her Britannic Majesty exactly as are Englishmen in the British Isles. . . .

"Cholon is something quite different. It ignores the West and has no desire to mingle with it, except in the night clubs—though even there the contact is only apparent and the dangers of contamination are reduced to a minimum. Cholon will teach you a great deal, if it is the Chinese mind and Chinese life you are interested in. But you'll have to rid yourself, as far as possible, of your Western concept. Besides, the Chinese hotel will help you do that."

My guide had chosen the Sun Wah, considering it to have the most strategic location, at the corner of the embankment and the most animated street in town. However, in order to get me into it a good deal of talking was necessary, for there is hardly room at a Chinese hotel for a permanent guest. It was much the same as asking for room and board in a brothel, except that here life was carried on, or at least seemed to be, in all openness.

Having finally prevailed, after a long confabulation in which I took no part, my companion took leave of me with a broad smile and the reverential bow, with hands joined. I found myself completely out of my element. And though life in an igloo had been a test for me, life here proved to be a greater and far more astonishing one.

How shall I describe the setting? Unlike the Western hotel, which is a place for lodging, the Chinese hotel is a place for living. It not only opens out—and opens widely —into the street, but is an extension of it. The lobby is a public place. Anyone at all may enter and install himself, women to nurse their babies on a comfortable bench in the shade, men to discuss business or idly watch the flow of people. The landing on each floor is a kind of town square, and the corridor into which the rooms empty is a street where people amble about with good humor and that apparently insatiable need of the Chinese to see and observe everything. The men stroll about, some in pajamas—the usual attire here—some bare-chested and in trousers, others in simple underpants, and all wearing the same kind of wooden sandals that resound through the hotel like clappers. The women stand in groups, chattering and laughing in high-pitched voices. The youngsters—most of them naked—dash about, then drop off to sleep right on the tiling, only to wake up again a moment later and resume their play.

The place is a town in itself, humming with noise, teeming with varied activity, reeking with odors that range from that of urine to the bitter smell of snakewood (which is burned to drive away mosquitoes), including the smells of hot fat, the sizzling innards of pigs—apparently a favorite delicacy—and the sweat of human beings. It is a true caravanserai where all human activities are carried on as freely as the heart desires, a place that is home, office, gambling den, washhouse, and brothel all rolled into one.

As my room was off the lobby, I had the impression of being on the bank of a swollen river. Never in all my life had I been so bewildered. Years before I had put in for a few days at Hong Kong, but that could scarcely be called participating in Chinese life. At present, all my notions about China were being knocked into a cocked hat. I had always thought the Chinese refined in their ways. But there they were all around me, wandering about half naked, wallowing everywhere, scratching their bellies or feet as casually as could be, spitting at random, urinating in the hall into a drain installed for that purpose. I had thought the Chinese were calm and phlegmatic. Yet as soon as there was the slightest discussion the tone mounted as if a dispute had broken out. I had thought they had an excessively keen sense of smell, yet the mixture of odors that I found nauseating left them utterly indifferent. I had thought them a silent people, but all around was an infernal racket, a din of high exclamations, clacking of mahjong tiles, screeching of phonographs that ground out Chinese music all about. And the people were not only untroubled by the noise but actually seemed to like it. I had thought the Chinese secretive, yet there at the hotel people ate and slept and fornicated in full view, as it were. And as for their being discreet, everybody was forever watching what was going on everywhere.

I had tried to take refuge in my room, if only long enough to regain self-possession, but that was quite impossible. To shut the door was contrary to ethics—and I was made to understand this very promptly. The door had to remain open as a sign of sociability.

My room, like all the others, was furnished very plainly, though ritualistically. Plainly, in that the walls were bare and there was almost nothing in the room. Ritualistically, in that the articles of furniture had a classic pattern. A flap-board bed with a thin mattress—in three parts—on a slat framework; a low, round table, flanked with four black wooden chairs, all enormously heavy; a wardrobe, extremely narrow; and a tiny washbasin with the merest trickle of water . . . when it flowed, for, so it appeared, there was no water three days out of six because of the dry season.

The cost of my room—fourteen hundred francs a day —seemed to me high, and I frankly expressed my surprise to my friend from Saigon the first chance I had.

"You don't understand!" he said. "You were introduced as a writer, and the man of letters is at the very top of the Chinese social hierarchy. He is even higher than the father, for 'though the father makes flesh, the scholar makes the spirit.' If they gave you a special rate, it was because they meant to honor you in accordance with your rank. They wouldn't have dared offend you by offering you a lower price!"

I did not know whether the explanation was correct. In

any case it was clever. And so when I was asked how I liked the Sun Wah, I could only declare that I was deeply gratified to have been admitted—though every morning I had to pay the day's bill. But that too, so it seemed, was the rule.

I must not fail to mention the other ritual objects contained in the room. On the table were three tiny teacups; on the shelf of the washstand, a red comb—red being the color of happiness; at the head of the bed, a fan-shaped fly swatter; under the bed, wooden-soled sandals. Then there was a vessel which, because of its shape, I took at first for a chamber pot. A handsome one, indeed, made of gleaming copper. "That's the most highly polished object in the entire setting!" I thought to myself, though the thing vaguely disturbed me.

The fact that the boyess would pull the pot from under the bed in the morning and set it under the table beside me simply increased my uneasiness. But I dared not protest. Her gesture—like that of first washing my cup by filling it with tea and then casually sprinkling the liquid about the room—was performed with the authority not only of a person who knew what she was about but also of one who meant to initiate you into the rites.

I had been made to understand from the very first day that if I wished to live there I had to conform to these rites. It was already quite clear that I would not have the right to a life of my own. Just as among the Eskimos it had been promptly made clear to me that my possessions, without exception, belonged to the group and that the group had a right to make use of them as it liked, similarly I would not be allowed to have privacy here. As long as I remained in my room the door was to re-

main open. All that protected me from being in full view
was the two panels, though as far as that went anyone
had the right to push them—a right that was fully ex-
ercised—to see what I was doing. This was not merely a
matter of idle curiosity but a way of saying: "You're one
of us!"

The sociability of the Chinese was becoming fully apparent to me. The guests of the hotel were constantly
visiting each other or chatting noisily in the corridor,
night and day alike, and with frequent bursts of laughter. Laughter meant good humor. Noise meant being
alive; and the more noise they made the happier they
seemed.

Whoever said the Chinese were a placid people? The
life about me wasn't merely intense, it was feverish. The
boyesses—as the female servants were called—would rush
from one compartment to the other. I say compartment,
for the rooms were "compartments for living" which a
person might rent for a few hours, whether to play a
game of mahjong or lie with a woman, or have friends
to supper, to the accompaniment of music. . . . And the
faster the boyesses ran the more the bell rang for them.
Someone was always wanting something. Here it was an
order for beer; there a call for the masseur, who would
turn up in a twinkling with his massage hammers. Elsewhere someone would be ordering food; there was no
mealtime, you ate when you were hungry. Farther off,
someone would send for a newspaper or a radio.

The boyesses responded to all calls not only with diligence and good humor but with all the authority inher-
ent in their status. They were not so much servants as
officiants. It was their job to keep up the rites, and—as

I was to see—everything in China is done in accordance with rites that are not to be violated. For example, each time I returned home it was the boyess who had to take the key from the board and precede me at a brisk pace so as to open the door of the room. Similarly, when I went out I could not close the door myself lest I be taken for a boor. That was the girl's job, and she did it as if it were a prerogative and not a chore.

On the other hand, I could not, without being insulting, ask the boyess to empty my spittoon (the object I had taken for a chamber pot, and a particularly useful one in that it also served as an ash tray and even a wastebasket). That is not part of her functions—I might almost say of her repertory. That is the charwoman's job.

I have always been struck, throughout the world, by the dignity, the high sense of duty, of the charwoman. I mean the one who works "by the hour" and goes from house to house with a consciousness of her role and a dignity in the performance of her work that makes of it a veritable "office"; who, wherever she goes to work, enters with authority and decision and sets about her business at once; who tolerates no nonsense, for she knows exactly what she has to do, and regards the home as a sacred place, the *domus* of the Latins. In her hands, not only the pots and pans but even the broom are ritualistic objects, for she confers a personality and a soul on the humblest of things. With her, everything becomes a matter of dialogue and exchange, of mutual enrichment. When she leaves, not only has the home taken on a polish but her face, too, is alight with something which, though indefinable, is nevertheless so apparent that people spontaneously make room for her in the bus.

"When you have seen one of those Chinese maids, you have seen them all. They walk quickly through the streets in their black silk trousers, pale blue jacket, carefully plaited braid and with the inevitable umbrella held in the middle . . ."

I observed the same phenomenon, though more sharply defined and more stylized, in Chinese maids. When you have seen one of them you have seen them all. They walk quickly through the streets in black silk trousers, pale blue jacket, carefully plaited braids, and with the inevitable umbrella held in the middle (they so resemble the attendants in the pagodas that you half expect them to be holding a string of Buddhist beads in the other hand).

The one who did my room—a wrinkled old woman with a face like a pippin—was a prodigy of diligence and, despite her age, of spriteliness. She would arrive at a set time, and it would have been useless to ask her to come back later: that was *her* hour! No sooner would she cross the threshold than she was mistress of the place. If I was writing she would remove the sheet of paper. And the sparkle of her square teeth as she laughed was so irresistible that it was impossible to be angry with her. She was an embodiment not only of the tirelessness and industriousness but also of the astonishing youthfulness of her people, who, though the most ancient in the world, have nevertheless retained an astonishing vitality.

III

ANOTHER aspect of Chinese vitality was revealed to me on the very evening of my arrival in Cholon, for the man who had introduced me to the manager of the Sun Wah had been so considerate as to invite me to dine at a restaurant with friends of his. "It will be a privilege for them," he said, "to meet the famous writer that you are. I assure you that they will be delighted." This was pure fabrication, but Chinese courtesy required that I be made to feel at ease.

However, for all his kindness, I still felt somewhat uncomfortable. I had, on an earlier occasion, in Hong Kong, experienced the peculiar politeness of the Chinese who, in swamping you with compliments, remain all the more elusive. The more delighted they declare themselves to meet you, the more uncomfortable you feel and the more aware you become that you are "a foreigner" and that it will take years for you to be "in"—if ever you are.

That evening, in Cholon, it was even worse, for it was apparent that my hosts saw only *their* universe. And I who, owing to my multifarious trials and tribulations, had something to offer, at least in conversation, in most gatherings, now felt as if I were an utter nonentity. I was like a layman dining with doctors, all of them heart specialists and interested only in heart ailments. Not that the atmosphere was hostile. China knows better than to be hostile to anyone. But her urbanity is that of a belly! The person who welcomes you heartily draws off your juices—he drains you chemically. The indifference of the Chinese to a foreigner—so long as he has not become his friend—is a strictly stomachal matter! Therein lies his force and his subtlety. Far from avoiding you, he offers himself, he is "entirely at your disposal," like a woman who, instead of resisting your advances, declares that she is indeed delighted with the dinner to which you have invited her, though at the end of the meal you are no further than you were before, and who, when you have brought her to her door, shakes your hand very sweetly and says, "Do ring me up one of these days." So long as the Chinese does not know you he will offer everything —and give nothing.

There were four of them that evening, all smothering me with compliments. How lucky they were to have met me! Was I comfortable at my hotel? Was it what I had wanted? They kept showering me with questions, and my answers were unfailingly received with "Ho-hos!" and "Ha-hahs!"—all very warm and friendly, though indicating no less warmly that they found me quite stupid. That sharp and inescapable sensation of having, in the course of a dinner, been "weighed and found wanting," is indeed one of the most uncomfortable I know.

Yet my hosts were not lacking in politeness or consideration. "Does the food please you? Would you care for more?" Despite this, however, I was discovering, in addition to the consideration of the Chinese, his offhandedness, or rather the perfect freedom with which, after performing the rites of courtesy, he starts "functioning," without further ado. For though they had welcomed me most ceremoniously and waited for me to pick up my chopsticks and serve myself, no sooner had I made the gesture than, without transition, they let themselves go and went at it—a veritable unloosing of insects! They stretched out their arms, now to one, now to the other of the numerous bowls on the table, and poked about with their chopsticks, which, as manipulated by them, seemed rather to be the feelers of insects. Here they would snap up a watermelon pit, there a bamboo shoot floating in the soup, then a fish bladder from a bowl. It was a masterly set-to-partners, a most elegant crisscross. At least it seemed so to me, for these prolongations of their fingers found their mark with prodigious sureness and skill. Though the rhythm accelerated, the sticks never collided or got in each other's way. And while puffing away—for they did puff hard—my companions would say, "Do take some of this! It's good, you'll see!" or "Plunge this duckling wing into that bowl of vinegar. That's what it's there for!"

I kept staring at the dishes. They contained such a variety of food that I wondered what each could possibly be. There were lots of green things, pale green, sea green, yellow green, and others tending toward violet, all of it as fibrous, sticky, or spongy as could be desired. The sticky stuff was the duck; the fibrous, the Chinese vermicelli and the swallows' nests; the spongy, the fish bladders. As for the glaucous spheres that kept staring at me, I presently learned that they were "hundred-year-old eggs" that had been steeped in ammonia and the yellow of which had turned black, a gummy black. The sight of them made me uneasy, as did the taste, for though there was something delicate about the flavor, it was also somewhat mawkish, slightly effeminate. They were followed immediately—the table kept filling up without anyone's seeming to order—by a variety of reeking dishes, the innards of pigs and duck gizzards (two creatures particularly prized by the Chinese because they are particularly nourishing). My table mates were tearing away avidly. And I, who even in the normal course of things would have had difficulty keeping up with them, was further incapacitated by an attack of hiccoughs which had started at the beginning of the meal. It was a violent attack, which, for all my efforts, I was unable to repress or conceal, and it contributed no little to my discomfort. Whereas *they*—they exulted at the sight of the food as did my Eskimos in the Great North at the sight of steaming seal. And though *I* was inadequate, they, on the other hand, pitched into the food unceremoniously, snapping up a duck tongue, fishing out a blade of seaweed and, in passing, a red pepper. They had long since stopped bothering about me. Having set out before the guest all that politeness required, they went at it with a will, and I, in the presence of this display of vitality, this rising exaltation, wondered anxiously how I was going to find my way in Chinese life.

It was clear that I had not yet "caught on." Now, with the Chinese, it is essential that you catch on. With them, as with the Eskimos, it is absolutely imperative that you be a jolly good fellow. You must demonstrate—and vigorously too—that you like everything they like. Similarly, you must not be repelled by certain of their ways, such as constant spitting, even in company, or extracting from one's mouth, with the help of the chopsticks, which act as dental pliers, bits of bone and other unassimilable parts of the food, and then laying them delicately on the tablecloth. In like manner it was quite natural to have as spectator at our meal—and also as fellow guest—a skeleton-like beggar with a foul breath who patiently watched the progress of our revels. Hardly would we finish a dish than he would stretch out his arm, take hold of what remained, pour it—meat, sauce, and all— into a screw of old newspaper and eat it then and there. In China begging is not only tolerated—it would be unseemly to chase away a poor man who was merely waiting—but it is regarded as one of the branches of human activity. At most, someone might say to you, "*A'pin in* [Opium]," to explain the individual's fleshlessness. But he would never dream of being huffy in his presence. In China, as long as you do not jostle your neighbor, you are free.

Finally, after two hours, the bout was over. My hosts drove me back to my hotel, for though it was only about a hundred yards away etiquette required that they do so. And after taking leave of me with much bowing and scraping they went off, probably to continue the evening elsewhere.

33

IV

THOUGH Cholon is an important city—according to statistics, the population is 650,000—nevertheless, this town of merchants and petty shopkeepers is far from having the glamor of Hong Kong or Singapore. It has no skyscrapers, no "banking district," none of those sumptuous colonnaded buildings that are in such striking contrast with the alleys all about them. Cholon is a low, flat town, sunk for the most part in dust, on the shores of a river called the Arroyo. The Arroyo has several arms. At times it is a river, at times a canal, with miles of dusty docks and innumerable hog-backed bridges. It is the chief artery of the town's life. All the goods and supplies that enter Cholon from the north, and even from China (for, despite the closing of the frontiers, mysterious exchanges take place between the two countries) flow down this river.

To begin with, there is rice. Wherever the Chinese may be, they control the rice, from its production to its distribution. If they wished to, they could starve all of Indo-China. Throughout the Orient the Chinese is the purveyor. He is the born businessman, a middleman to the core of his being, who will provide you with any-thing—women, spices, opium, or smuggled weapons. He is also the purveyor. And all the products that reach Cholon after a slow journey are stored up in countless warehouses (the Chinese name for Cholon is T'ai Ngon, which means, roughly, "the steps by the dock"). I was once told that if anyone ever knew what was accumu-lated in Cholon, and the more or less hidden reserves it contained, he would be utterly staggered. In fact the Chinese is a man who will always dig out something more from his shop, and then still more . . . if he wants to. Does he lack the article you require? He'll send some-one to get it elsewhere while he chats with you. In short his shop is bottomless, or rather, the bottom is all China!

Having said this, I should add that Cholon has not the picturesqueness of certain Chinese cities. One must not expect to find there the Street of Gold or the Lane of the Mortuary Wreaths or the streaming banners that give certain cities their magical and concretely mysteri-ous character. Cholon is nevertheless a teeming city. The street is in a state of constant bustle, suggesting the busy coming and going of an anthill. And the denser the crowd the more content the Chinese feel. They like to be together. For them, business and the pleasures of society go hand in hand.

However teeming the Chinese crowd may be, it re-mains curiously orderly. Indeed, the spirit of crowds dif-fers from country to country. Take the German crowd. It follows its standard or its chief. It is the latter who leads—and hypnotizes—it. Or take the Spanish crowd. God knows that its members are restless and passionate, but their passion is individual. Even in a crowd the Spaniard is alone, strangely wrapped up in himself. The Near Eastern crowd, on the other hand, is essentially collective. It is an electrically charged body that can be inflamed by the merest trifle. Not at all so the Chinese crowd. In certain ways it reminds me of the English crowd, which does not jostle, in which each person moves in accordance with his neighbor. The Chinese retains his urbanity, even in a crowd. Self-contained though he be, he has nevertheless a high sense of his relations with the outside world and of human intercourse, a sense that is the product of age-old training. He is a man with a peculiar gift for creating an atmosphere of amiability, for facilitating contacts and smoothing out difficulties, for maintaining the "communication" that is the basis of his entire philosophy. He is thus the most sagacious of shopkeepers and the subtlest of diplomats. For him nothing is impossible. Just as no deal is without interest, so everything is worth while. He is a born artist in human relations. And he is also the *comprador* who buys for you and finds you a market, the intermediary who substitutes for you in handling transactions so that you need not lose face in case of failure. He is a man capable of obtaining anything for you through his contacts. His great strength lies in mutual aid. The links among Chinese make up a network that covers the globe. To render a Chinese a service is to set off a chain reaction the ramifications of which would leave you dumbfounded—if ever you discovered them.

I had been told about all this in advance. The

Chinese, I was informed, is capable of everything if he takes a liking to you. It is not a matter of a *casual* liking, of a burst of friendly feeling that is promptly forgotten. No. The Chinese is the most cautious man in the world when it comes to giving of himself, and the most mistrustful. In relations with him there is a threshold that must first be crossed, and, until it is, nothing will happen. Behind the politeness, which is all convention, he will be scrutinizing you to your very marrow. Your most insignificant gesture will be noted. The merest contraction of your face will be subjected to a sharp examination—and the Chinese is a past master in physiognomy. Without suspecting it, you will be under constant observation. Then, one fine day the doors will open wide, without your quite understanding what it was that led to the decision. For the Chinese has his mystery and that is not the least of his charms.

Let us return to the street, for it is in the street, or at doorsteps, that most things take place. The street is his shop and living room, his playground, observation post, and almost everything else. Take that inconspicuous young woman walking through the crowd just a few steps ahead of an old servant woman. She is a hetaera. But you must not approach her. She would lose face. And so would you if she declined your offer. It is to the woman following her that you must address yourself to discuss, in discreet fashion, the possibility, the price, and other details. . . . Or that old man floating along, with his eyes half closed, as if in a dream, with the sparse hairs of his mustache falling in the ancient manner. He is a scholar taking his daily stroll in white silk pajamas and felt slippers. . . . Those three men scurrying along in

"*That old man floating along, with his eyes half closed, as if in a dream, with the sparse hair of his mustache falling in the ancient manner. He is a scholar taking his daily stroll in white silk pajamas and felt slippers . . .*"

single file with their musical instruments under their arms are performers who have been summoned to some private establishment to entertain clients. . . . That man sitting against the wall with a deck of cards spread out between his legs is a fortuneteller. . . . And that one over there walking along the curb and shaking coins in a metal cylinder—it gives off a very particular sound—is the masseur. You need only beckon and he will come to your room to relax your tired muscles.

That chap farther off who has just dismounted from his bicycle and leaned it against a tree, and who is tacking a little mirror onto the trunk, is the itinerant barber. All his equipment is in a box on his baggage rack. Not only will he cut your hair but, upon request, he will remove the wax from your ears, scrape your nostrils, and clean the backs of your eyelids! . . . The street trades are legion. Nearby is a man who, with a wheel that he turns with one arm and one leg, will crush young bamboo to extract a juice that he will serve you in a glass. A few yards farther off a cobbler squats on the sidewalk, operating with equipment that fits into the three drawers of a portable case. Up the street is a scissor grinder sharpening instruments with a long stone. To make known his presence he rattles his Chinese scissors, for each trade has its own noise, which announces that such and such a specialist is going by. One man shakes his key ring. Another rings his bell. A third, with a flick of the wrist, shakes a ball that strikes a drum, setting up a raking sound that can be heard from a distance.

The women are more discreet. The cigarette woman sits motionless behind her stand, as do the small-ware dealers behind their showcases, letting their silk spools and other articles speak for themselves with their shimmering colors. The same for the woman who sells fish for home aquariums. The beauty of her wares, Siamese fighting fish, blue-green fish with feathered wings, is sufficient to attract one's eye.

And then there are the semipermanent stalls, which are set up on the sidewalk opposite the shops in such a way as to leave a narrow lane between the two. These, with their displays of food, are the most picturesque of all: bamboo sprouts, so tender-green that they make your mouth water, lines of lacquered ducks hanging from hooks, weirdly twisted innards of pigs, and translucent fish bladders. That's where one eats best, and cheapest. All day long and part of the night clients sit around these counters and nibble at their snacks in the most casual postures while watching the crowd go by. When time for siesta comes round the dealer shuts up shop, puts the food under the floor boards, and sleeps . . . on the counter, with his entire family. At about four o'clock this little world comes to life again. The stalls are again garlanded with food as if by enchantment and are in full glory until far into the night.

The mere street spectacle is enough to reveal the qualities of this people. They are ingenious and can turn the merest trifle into a gala. Their mastery of the art of display borders on wizardry. And they are very deft and incomparably light-fingered. And hard-working, too, despite appearances. They have a profound sense of humor, and at the same time are philosophers to their fingertips. And, withal, keen observers, able to size you up at once and anticipate your wishes.

What is most striking of all is that they are satisfied

with the barest of necessities. Never have I seen human beings make shift with so little. With four boards a Chinese can set up a business; with three implements he is ready to practice a trade. As for vital space, a bit of sidewalk a yard and a half square is enough for a Chinese to set up shop and to live in it with his entire family, which is generally a large one, for his code prescribes that he have at least five children. At closing time, which is often at three in the morning, they fold up on the spot. As the length of the shelter is less than that of a man, their legs—and at times their heads—dangle out. Not that they find such a way of life comfortable, but they have an infinite capacity for putting up with things. Although lacking comfort, they have a store of wisdom and they know how to derive a deep pleasure from trifles. It is no uncommon thing to see a shabby beggar standing by a wall and removing his rags to revel in the last rays of the sun.

And how mobile they are! Although time and again I tried to sketch them, I got nowhere. Every image—and feeling—is incredibly fleeting. Only the swiftness of the camera can catch it. But the camera cannot really render it, for each expression reveals a world. And it is replaced by another in a fraction of a second.

Another thing that makes drawing "from life" almost impossible is the curiosity of the Chinese, which he cannot resist. If, for example, the boyess at the hotel found me reading, she would take the book from my hands to inspect it more closely. In the street, no sooner would I reach into my pocket for my pencil and notebook than I would be surrounded by a dozen spectators eager to see

42

what I was doing, and all the more intrigued by my drawing in that my visual sensibility was not theirs. For as long as I sketched they would stand about, consumed by curiosity.

V

My second Chinese dinner, which, like the first, was organized by local friends, took place at the home of Mr. Chang. Mr. Chang was an acupunctor. At least, that was his chief profession, for the Chinese of Cholon frequently have several irons in the fire, and at first sight their activities seem to have nothing in common. Do you want to have a book bound? Then you must see the barber, who is also a bookbinder. In like manner, you will discover that the local carpenter is also . . . a dentist. Would you like to know how he gets his training? By yanking out, with thumb and forefinger, pegs that are driven more and more deeply into blocks of wood. As a result, he can extract your molar without forceps!

Mr. Chang's home was strategically situated in the busiest section of Cholon, opposite one of the permanent street markets. His home, like almost all in town, was composed of a first room that was both living and dining room, adorned—not to say cluttered—with ritual em-

blems, the chief of which was the ancestors' altar opposite
the entrance. The room was at street level. Thus, at mealtime, passers-by could see the tenants, often dressed only
in shorts, sitting on their haunches about a table and
going at their food with gusto.

Mr. Chang's main room was also adorned with an enlarged colored photograph of his father, who had also
been an acupunctor, and with anatomical plates, likewise in color, showing the different "canals" of human
energy, in accordance with the theory of acupuncture.

The next room served as the doctor's consulting room.
It contained a row of cots, on one of which lay the person whom the doctor was treating. I watched him work.
He gently dug his needle into the patient's back, where
the left sympathetic nerve was located. After a brief
pause he dug it in a little more deeply. Then he paused
again and, this time with a sharp thrust, drove the needle
all the way in, vertically.

Leaving the needle in position, he took a second one
and operated in the same way, on a level with the first
but at the right sympathetic. He left the two needles in
place for about three minutes, then withdrew them with
a sharp jerk. At the site of the puncture he applied a
ringlet which he had cut out of the greenish tuber of a
plant. This was done to stop the flow of blood.

Having sent the patient off, he then turned to me. Mr.
Chang was a stocky man, with a powerful torso, who did
his job very briskly. His laughter—he was forever laughing—was the characteristic laughter of the Chinese.
There is no telling whether it indicates politeness, good
humor, guile, or all three.

As Mr. Chang knew no foreign language, the friends

who had brought me explained who I was. This provoked a display of mimicry on the part of the doctor that
left me bewildered, particularly as Mr. Chang's upper
jaw was protuberant, like that of many Chinese, with the
result that every time he laughed his teeth spread
fanwise.

I ought to have responded to this rush of civilities by
one equally animated, but, alas, I was unable to. We
then sat down to eat. The table was set, though I had
not noticed the slightest movement; everything had been
brought from the restaurant across the street. This was
typical of Chinese mutual assistance. If you lack anything
at home your servant rushes out to borrow it from a
neighbor. This kind of thing is done without giving it a
second thought.

There were five of us at the table, all men (the women
never appear unless you are very close friends). One of
the guests was the editor in chief of the most important
local newspaper, a militant fellow with sunken cheeks,
who expressed his views very violently. His neighbor, who
was a newspaperman too—though he also ran a laundry!
—was a round-faced chap whose skin was as smooth and
gleaming as if it had been smeared with fresh butter. It
was he who had presented me at the Sun Wah. The last
was the very type of the intellectual. His hair stood up
stiff and straight, like chopsticks. His teeth stuck out of
his mouth. And he had a curiously prominent Adam's
apple. He told me that he was an English translator in
Saigon. It was he who acted as interpreter during the
meal. But his Chinese accent was so strong that his
English was incomprehensible. But what did it matter!
The thing that counted was the atmosphere. Since we

47

"*The last of the guests was the very type of the intellectual. His hair stood up stiff and straight, like chopsticks; his teeth stuck out of his mouth.*"

were among "men of letters," it was bound to be good.

At first we drank a small glass of rice brandy, a traditional drink. I occupied the seat farthest from the street door, having been so placed because of the evil spirits, whereas our host was seated nearest to the door in order to ward off a possible invasion.

Once again I had to pick up my chopsticks and give the signal to go ahead. Once again I observed the incredible vitality of the Chinese and the gusto with which he tackles whatever he does. Immediately my fellow guests swooped down on the fried crab, plunging it with a side stroke into a bowl of soya extract. Then they went at the fish bladders, then the roast squab, adding, according to their individual fancy, such and such an ingredient from one of the bowls. . . . The rhythm began to accelerate. Arms shot forward; pincers snapped up with equal dexterity and eagerness a nut or bamboo shoot or lettuce leaf. They would interrupt themselves only long enough to say to me, "Take some! You ought to taste it. It's good!"

But I was no longer hungry. Their digital acrobatics, bordering on frenzy, had dizzied me. It was not only a matter of appetite. What was going on before my eyes was something deeper and more subtle, a satisfying not only of the taste buds but of the whole being, the contentment of the man who, having materialized his concept perfectly, is capable of delighting in it endlessly.

Finally the frenzy subsided. Though I had long ceased to be anything but a spectator, they were not at all embarrassed. Once the Chinese has let himself go he discards all ceremoniousness, and he expects you to do likewise. Any stiffness on your part would be impoliteness.

I would have liked, since I had the good fortune to be at the home of a doctor, to question Mr. Chang about his profession, but it was obvious that he had not the slightest desire to be questioned, just as he was not tempted to question me. Nothing interested him except China. The Chinese have a feeling of superiority to other races that is glaringly obvious. It is not a matter of arrogance, as with certain nations, but rather of conviction. As for trying to make a Chinese talk when he doesn't want to! You must arm yourself with patience; if you don't you're licked. Moreover I had been warned about this. The only way of getting anything out of a Chinese is to be more Chinese than he—if you can. If he is not in a hurry, you must be even less so. Do you feel irritated? You must hasten to say that, as far as you are concerned, all is for the best in the best of all possible worlds.

I finally ventured to ask Mr. Chang whether he would care to diagnose me. He burst out laughing, as if it were the most incongruous of questions. In a twinkling he changed the subject. "These people know how to handle themselves," I thought to myself. "They have a way of slipping between your fingers so that you can't even be angry with them."

However, a half hour later the interpreter said to me, "Mr. Chang is going to examine you."

My host stood up with a suddenly mysterious air and went to get a small table on which was a low swivel lamp. He requested me to be seated, took my left hand, and placed it, palm upward, on a small embroidered cushion. Then he placed his three fingers on the vein of my wrist. I watched him. His eyes were lost in reverie, as if his mind were far away, while his fingers tapped very lightly over the surface of my skin.

I knew what he was trying to do, to bring his own sensibility into focus. He first had to make contact. Chinese medicine, like our Hippocratic medicine of old, attaches extreme importance to this "communication" between doctor and patient. I also recalled certain old works which speak of the knowledge of the universe, the "information" that reaches us through our extremities. Hence the importance that palmists attach to the form of the fingers.

Mr. Chang kept tapping away. Not only his fingers but his entire being grew more and more feverish.

Suddenly his fingers stopped moving. He had made contact! Nothing stirred in the room. Absolute quiet was essential so that the operator could function. The entire room seemed to be waiting spellbound. If this was play acting, they were doing an excellent job.

I myself believed in the Chinese pulse. But did the others? Impossible to tell. One of the enthralling things about the Chinese is that you never know whether he believes in the rites he performs so zealously.

Suddenly Mr. Chang's fingers pressed a bit harder. He was seeking the intermediate pulses, those halfway down.[1] There was a pause. Then, suddenly, as if swooping on an elusive prey, he pressed hard.

---

[1] The Chinese distinguish nine pulses in each wrist, three surface pulses, three intermediate pulses, and three deep-seated pulses; thus, eighteen in all, each of which corresponds to a specific organ.

The operation was repeated with my right wrist. Following this, Mr. Chang swung his light on me.

"Show me your tongue."

From my tongue he looked into my eyes, studied the corners of my mouth. I submitted to the examination in silence, for I knew that the Chinese doctor is able to make a complete diagnosis on the basis of the pulse and facial appearance alone. For him, the eyes, ears, nostrils, mouth, and so on are all "windows." The color of the skin is also observed. He pays particular attention to odors as indications of "humors," and to the exhalations of the skin, which vary, according to him, with the individual's state of health. The Chinese doctor observes even the tone of the voice, the slightest alteration in which is revealing.

Finally Mr. Chang spoke.

"How old are you?" he asked through the interpreter.

I replied in the Chinese manner: "How old does Mr. Chang think I am?"

"Thirty-eight to forty."

I was unable to hold back a smile. "I'm fifty-four."

Mr. Chang started.

"He says it's not possible!" explained the interpreter.

Mr. Chang's incredulity flattered me. Besides, I was somewhat pleased to have caught a Chinese doctor in error.

Mr. Chang glanced at me rapidly. But I had obviously spoken the truth. His expression changed. Then he muttered a few words rapidly and the interpreter translated.

"Mr. Chang says in that case you have a magnificent pulse!"

"What else?"

"You will never have tuberculosis. The only organ you have to be careful about is your liver."

I nodded. I knew that my liver behaved erratically. "Have you," I asked, "any herbs for the liver?"

"We have herbs for everything."

Mr. Chang stood up and went to get a book, which he opened and showed to me. It was a treatise on Chinese pharmacopoeia and contained an entire nomenclature of plants . . . including coral! Each plant was described; also indicated were its Latin name, the various names given to the plant in the different provinces of China, the different varieties and the places in China where they were to be found, the theoretical qualities of the plant, and its practical applications and the results that could be expected from its use. Lastly there was the list of organs which the plant affected and the ailments which it could remedy.

I took leave of Mr. Chang with all the thanks and bows that the ceremonial required.

But it was clear that if I hoped to enter into the Chinese mind I first had to learn to speak Chinese. The Chinese would not come to me: I therefore had to go to them.

VI

But how was I to go about learning Chinese? What was the best approach? My Chinese-speaking friends in Saigon were not of the same mind about how to proceed, for there were two possible policies, one immediate, the other long-range.

"The only thing for you to do," said one of them, "is to learn the spoken language. There's no need to burden yourself with studying the written language. It has ten thousand characters, each of which is an ideogram. You'll never master it in a year. Learn Cantonese. That's the language of Cholon. It's relatively easy. Here's a good method." And he handed me a book.

A second friend had a different point of view. "If," he said, "all De Poncins wants during his stay in Cholon is to be able to get along in the street and in the shops, the spoken language is sufficient. But if it's the Chinese concept that he's interested in, the Chinese way of thinking, the spoken language is not enough. He won't get anywhere. It won't give him the 'key.' To be sure, a study of the characters and the initiation it requires involve considerable effort, especially at the beginning. But even if he learns only very little, that little will reveal to him more about the Chinese soul than all the rest." And he set before me a pile of dictionaries—Aubenzac, Matthews, Wieger—all of them familiar to Sinologists.

As soon as I opened them I became aware of the enormousness of the task, for the Chinese character—the key characters, of which there are several hundred, must be learned by heart before one can go any further—is not a word but an ideogram. Each of them expresses an idea or group of ideas that are related to one another, first pictorially, then phonetically, then symbolically. This is a world in itself, one utterly different in concept from ours. Hence, before learning the signs, one must necessarily assimilate the concept.

At this stage of my perplexity a third man spoke up and complicated everything. "Not only will a smattering of the spoken language not get our friend anywhere, at least anywhere important, but it will handicap him considerably when he wants to start learning the written language, for if he uses a dictionary in Roman characters he will be retaining the Western concept that he must get rid of at any cost if he wants to understand China."

I seemed to be getting nowhere. The solution would be to find a Chinese teacher. But how could I make myself understood if he spoke no other tongue, as seemed to be the case of the Chinese here? Although I spoke eight languages, they would be of no use to me.

"Nevertheless," said one of my friends, "we'll see whether we can find someone for you."

But as nothing is done directly in China, it was necessary to get in touch with certain friends who, in turn, would pass the request on to others. This would take time.

But my problem was an immediate one; I had to know enough Chinese to be able to get along at the hotel, for despite the graciousness—tinged ever so slightly with a spirit of mischief—the fact is that I was not getting along. Take breakfast, for example. They brought me tea, but it was thin and watery, whereas I like it strong. How was I to explain what I wanted? If I made a sign indicating that it was unsatisfactory, they were very surprised and took it away only to return a moment later with tea that was just as weak.

I finally put up with the weak tea, but at least I would have liked sugar and milk. Without realizing it, I was offending against the etiquette. Had I asked for a prostitute, that would have been in the normal order of things. But not this! They made it quite clear to me, though pretending not to understand what I wanted. When I asked for sugar—I finally learned the word for it—they took away the tea and returned with sugar in a saucer, but no tea! And the girl stood there, with a somewhat bantering smile, to see what I was going to do with it. They had a way all their own of making fun of me and, though all smiles, of trying my patience. But had I shown irritation I would have lost face, and then all would have been lost. I ended by going to the kitchen, excusing myself with a smile—the kitchen was an incredible cavern!—and helping myself to the ingredients I wanted, which provoked a flowering of grins.

57

I had to learn Chinese, if only to live. I headed for Saigon and returned with a *Beginner's Handbook of the Cantonese Language.*

But even there a difficulty arose from the very start, that of the "Chinese tones." In Cantonese, for every word, however simple, there are nine tones. These tones were indicated in the handbook, but by more or less cabalistic signs.

Then there are the "lower" tones and the "upper" tones and, in each of these categories, the "horizontal" tone, the "brief ascending tone," the "brief descending tone," the "long ascending tone," and the "long descending tone." And each word takes on a very different meaning, depending on the tone.

I picked a word at random, the word *fu.* It means, depending on the tone: husband, dignitary—attend, support—bitter, hard, rot—tiger—palace, residence—verbal order—father—mother, woman—happiness.

Would I ever learn to differentiate them by mere elocution? There were nuances that, to a Western ear, were almost imperceptible. Therefore my ear first required a completely new education. So did the larynx, for how was one to pronounce the character *M,* indicating negation? And the character *tsz,* representing "business"? Only a Chinese tutor could teach me.

And even the spoken language, however simple it might be compared to the written, presented innumerable complications. For example, in Chinese everything must be "qualified" very precisely. One does not say: *yat ok* (a house) but *yat kaan ok* (a—divided into compartments—house). Not *yat shue* (a book) but *yat poun shue* (a—source, origin—book). Not *yat shaan* (a mountain) but *yat tso shaan* (a—base, pedestal—mountain). Every noun requires a qualifier immediately preceding it.

So the only thing for me to do was to learn these qualifiers by heart. For curiosity's sake, I list them as given in my manual:

Fai   For boards and, in general, whatever is flat.

Fou   For coffins and any article manufactured on a large scale.

Foung   For letters.

Ka   For automobiles, machines.

Kaan   For homes, buildings, and whatever is compartmentalized.

Ko   For men and whatever is ill determined.

Kwoh   For countries, nations.

Nap   For grains, buttons, stars.

Pa   For fans, umbrellas, scissors (for anything that closes within itself).

Poun   For books and all printed matter.

Tat   For places.

Tchek   For animals, arms, legs, dishes, boats.

Tcheung For sheets of paper, tables, chairs, blankets.

Tchi   For branches (and whatever has a stemlike form).

Ten   For hats (and summits in general).

Teuh   For flowers, flames (whatever blazes).

Tin   For the time of day, points, drops.

Tiou   For streets, rivers, fish, snakes (whatever is long and thin, whatever flows and winds).

To   For doors, bridges (whatever is a passageway).

Tso   For mountains, cities, pagodas.

Wai   For honorable persons.

59

Thus it is apparent that the Chinese assembles things which, for us, are very different from each other, but in which he sees a similarity of form. I therefore first had to acquire a concrete, yet figurative, view of the universe.

Meanwhile I drank my fill of the spectacle of the hotel. In order to observe it there was no need for me to leave my room, as my door, in accordance with etiquette, remained open. I had only to push one of the two swinging doors that blocked the view halfway up. The lobby was constantly crowded with guests, visitors, and friends all chatting away. Here, for example, comes a prostitute whom someone has been sent to get at her home. If ever one wants a girl he is given the sheaf of paper that hangs from a nail in the office, each sheet of which contains the name of one of the prostitutes employed by the hotel, with her physical description and an indication of her special talents. Preceded by the boyess, she glides through the crowd of idlers with the dignity and reserve befitting her office. As she passes, she smiles at the bookkeepers who, on each floor, go over their accounts in a narrow space separated from the rest of the lobby by a kind of counter. They do their calculations with a Chinese abacus, an instrument which, primitive though it be, does not only addition but multiplication and division, and the speed with which they perform their operation is not surpassed by that of the most modern machines. Then there are the "old women" who go by imperturbably, carrying a broom or a rag. There are also the boys, in white jackets and black trousers, always ready to dash, even outside the hotel. I would meet them in the street, looking very busy and mysterious, ready to perform any service whatever. There are the friends who come for a game of mahjong. Mahjong is played on every floor and at all times of the day, except during siesta. There is the barber who walks down the corridor, rattling his scissors to make known his presence. There are the guests who, likewise at all hours of the day, go to the showers at the end of the corridor. Only one of the five stalls works, and it is constantly occupied, sometimes by a woman wiping her child clean or another doing her laundry. Here one is completely free.

When the dinner hour comes round, the boys and boyesses take their places at a round table right in the middle of the lobby. From the kitchens, unbelievably primitive with their simple fire-clay stoves, which are set right on the floor (they look less like kitchens than steaming caverns where greasy, bare-chested boys rush about like demons), come bowls of rice and reeking entrails of pigs.

At night it is also in the middle of the lobby that the boys and boyesses set up the stretchers that serve as their beds. However, no sooner would they lie down than they would spring from the canvas because a guest had rung. One of them wants beer—at three in the morning, for what with chatter, gambling, and women the Chinese stays up late. Another asks for a girl; he has suddenly felt like having one, and the Chinese does not resist his desires.

One thing that is apparent in all this spectacle is the intense need of the Chinese to live, to "function," and also his instinct of sociability. The Chinese does not care for solitude; he regards it as something unhealthy. Two things in particular are inconceivable to him, and even suspect: to live alone and to resist desires. As soon as I arrived at the hotel—and even before I opened my valises—I was offered a girl, and the hotel people were quite astonished that I did not want one. Isn't it agreeable to have a girl at one's side, even if only to take pleasure in contemplating her figure if she is beautiful? The Chinese is essentially a man who knows how to take pleasure in things, whether it be a well-cooked dish, the skin of a woman, the feel of jade, or the color of a fish. He relishes one as intensely as the other. They are all part of a whole. According to him, it is not possible to disassociate pleasures. Such and such a delight is not to be isolated. Just as tasty dishes are not enough to make a good Chinese dinner—it also requires the charm of politeness, courtesy, the pleasure of conversation, the presence, if possible, of pretty girls and musicians—so Chinese eroticism cannot be confined to love. It is multifarious and can be as keen about the flavor of a dish as the sight of a rare object or the fragrance of a flower. One feeling is dominant in the Chinese make-up, one that explains him perhaps more completely than anything else: his love of form.

VII

THE spectacle that made me understand the Chinese
sense of form, the innate feeling for form not only for its
own sake but as the manifestation of a deeper beauty,
was, more than anything else, the theater, to which I
was taken by Chinese friends (they always escorted me
in a group of three or four).

The particular theater to which I was taken, though
the leading one in town—it is there that the greatest
actors of China itself perform when they are on tour—is
located in a narrow street. To get to it one has to worm
one's way through the clutter of pushcarts of the fritter
vendors and hawkers of other delicacies who set up shop
in front of the entrance. Also in front of the entrance is
usually a crowd of folk too poor to buy tickets but content to get a whiff of the show from afar, for seats are expensive. They cost about nine dollars and are not even
armchairs, but mere flap seats. Even at that price it is

no easy matter to get them, for a large number of the tickets are sold on the black market.

The lobby was adorned with huge banners containing large Chinese characters. One of my friends, paying no attention to the long line, went straight to the box office and asked for five tickets, which he was given instantly, because the ticket seller knew *who* he was. (In China everybody knows who you are.) He was a man of letters, hence an important figure, escorting what was a rare bird for Cholon, an Occidental.

We entered. The hall was likewise adorned with streamers everywhere, some pasted to the walls and others hanging from the ceiling; in addition, just above the stage curtain was the "votive streamer," which places the troupe, wherever it goes, under the protection of *its* divinity.

The crowd was so dense that we had a hard time forcing our way through. But nobody grumbled. Amiability was the rule—even more than amiability, for when we got to the first row of the orchestra, and the usher who was guiding us said a few words to the people seated there, they stood up and, all smiling, gave us their seats. Where else could one see such a thing? Could anyone imagine spectators in a Paris or New York theater giving up the seats for which they had paid so dearly to newcomers simply because they were escorting a foreigner? One can imagine the protests, the sarcastic comments! But here the gesture was utterly natural.

The show had been on for some time when we arrived, but as the Chinese play lasts a good four hours and as the public is already familiar with it, people quite commonly go to the theater only for an hour or

two just to steep themselves in the atmosphere. Moreover, the Chinese never tire of seeing the same plays, if
only to examine the fine points or observe how the same
role is handled by different actors.

There were only two actresses on the stage at the moment. They were wearing costumes—of the Great Age,
as always—thick with tinsel, some of it embroidered
and some laid on. Despite this, the costumes looked so
light that the players had an air of cherry trees in
bloom. I was even more struck, however, by their make-
up. Whereas Western actors use make-up to heighten
their features, on the Chinese stage it becomes a mask,
red and creamy white. The white covers the entire fore-
head and bridge of the nose. The rest of the face, from
the eyebrows down, is red, as is the neck, and the color-
ing shades off as it descends. The palms are also painted
red, and the fingernails are silvered over. The effect is
most striking. Thus each of the actors has the mask of
his role. The "noble father" is rigged out in a huge
beard, mustaches drooping from both sides of the mouth,
and thick eyebrows, in order to look dignified and
majestic. The matron—played by a man disguised as a
woman—is a ponderous figure who walks with a waddle.
The make-up of the servant girls is intentionally crude,
with violent red smears on the cheeks. The one who
plays the scullery wench splotches her face with big
black patches that look like pustules. And what pains she
took—I went to see her on another occasion—disfiguring
herself in her dressing room!

The thing that struck me most about the actors' performance, as it could not fail to strike any newcomer to
the Chinese theater, was their mimicry, a mimicry highly

studied and formally exact, that expressed the whole range of the feelings the actors were supposed to be experiencing and that amplified them, if need be, for the benefit of the spectators. It was a true *commedia dell' arte,* quite perfect of its kind. And, as in the *commedia dell' arte,* where everything is suggested and represented symbolically, there was no need of a door to go from one room to another. The actor had merely to lift his leg high and take a big step to indicate that he had crossed a threshold. Mimicry alone made it unnecessary to change sets during the performance.

The following scene took place between one of the two actresses, who remained alone, and a new arrival, a young man. My right-hand neighbor explained the scene to me aloud, for in China people are not shy, and the people about us were too good-natured to protest. The scene, a classic one, was that of the poor but lettered boatman courting the rich girl. Social classes as we know them in the West do not exist in China. There are the rich and the poor, but here a poor man who is cultivated is treated with at least as much consideration as a rich one.

There was the scene, very elaborately worked out, in which the poor but lettered boatman arrived in his modest skiff to woo in secret the girl of the rich boat (of which all that could be seen was the prow, but the mere decoration indicated its elaborateness). The way in which the skiff emerged from the wings and moved across the stage would have made a Western audience laugh. The prop, which was merely a matter of painted cardboard, was pushed by two bare-chested stage hands with the aid of the boatman, who with his oar mimed

66

the rowing. The stage hands made not the slightest effort to conceal their presence. In China the audience has a right to see everything that goes on, in back as well as in front. And while watching the actors who are on the stage, it likes to see those who are waiting their turn leaning against the framework of a flat, as well as the stage hands who are about to come on and the musicians in shirt sleeves playing in a corner of the wings, for there is no orchestra pit (the music rather suggests that of our village choral societies).

At length, push by push, the boatman neared the handsome barge on which the girl of his dreams was standing. Whereupon there began between them a pantomime, an exchange of simperings, that lasted a good half hour but that was so rich in nuances that the spectators were absorbed from beginning to end. Moreover, in the Chinese theater the actors take their time. Every posture expresses a feeling, every gesture a shade of that feeling. And each gesture must be performed in accordance with classical rules, though this does not at all prevent the actor from having his personal style, and it is precisely the perfection of this style that the spectator comes to admire. Each actor allows his partner time to give his gesture its full value, to such a degree that the spectator expects at any moment to see one of them start all over again because the gesture he has just made was not quite perfect. And the audience would applaud such professional conscience.

And so the boatman was wooing his beloved, with all the gestures of humility appropriate to his state and also with the admiration that was only the fair one's due. At the same time he itemized—aside, for the benefit of the audience

67

—her charms, as if saying to the audience, "I should like to point out to you, in the event that you may not have noticed it, the perfection of her throat, the purity of line of her bosom." Here the audience was let into the secret, and the actor was constantly playing a double game, addressing now his partner, now the audience, in order to keep it abreast of his impressions. And there was no need for him to turn around. He simply gave his mouth a twist in order to show that he was going to utter a confidence. . . . Now he felt he was on the right path, and he so informed the audience with a gesture to let it know that "it's coming along fine!" He drew near to his beloved, prudently, made so bold as to take hold of her little finger. Whereupon the maiden, pretending to awaken from the torpor into which the compliments of her suitor had plunged her, expostulated violently by means of gestures, scolded him by gestures and, feigning wrath (all this involved a cunning gradation), struck him with her fan. The rash suitor jumped back, displaying all the signs of great pain, and, with fresh humility, immediately resumed his wooing.

All this was at times spoken, at times sung, in the Chinese manner, with a head voice and infinite modulations on the same theme. For the non-initiate, this was rather like caterwauling. But if one bears in mind that the Chinese language is monosyllabic, one will understand that there cannot be singing as we understand it, any more than there can be an orchestra in our sense of the terms. The orchestra, which is composed of five or six musicians—violin, flute, and brasses—is not there to blend with the singing but rather to indicate the emergence of a particular feeling or its intensity and color.

68

The violin is for the sighs of love, the brasses for anger; one clash of the brasses denotes a mere flash of anger, and three are for really strong anger. Meanwhile the actor indicates his wrath by gestures. Depending on the intensity he wishes to express, he shakes his head or kicks his heels violently on the floor.

There was one scene in the play that is worth relating in detail.

Two students, each holding an enormous brush so that there is no mistaking their identity, and of an age well beyond puberty (for the mere apprenticeship in the Chinese language requires seven years), are each seated at a table on either side of the stage and engaged very reluctantly in literary composition. One of them stretches, with all the signs of the most extreme weariness, while the other yawns wide enough to unhinge his jaw and wiggles his leg frantically under the table to show that he is in a state of utter exasperation. They are both racking their brains, but without success.

"I'm quite annoyed," says one. "My wife said that she wouldn't sleep with me tonight if I didn't write a poem to her."

The other replies with a gesture indicating that he is not making any headway either.

They flounder about that way for a good ten minutes, to the delight of the audience, and grow increasingly restless until one of them topples over backward while making a motion to show that his brain is completely empty, and the other collapses on his desk, nose first. One of them seems indifferent to the fact that he is making no progress; the other, however, shows that the desire to sleep with his wife is turning him topsy-turvy.

At this point, along comes the lettered boatman, quite nonchalant and very sure of himself. From the traditional lackey's outfit that he is now wearing, the audience gathers that he has succeeded in obtaining employment as a servant in the home of the girl he loves. After a great display of feigned excuses he asks what is wrong.

"Ah!" exclaimed the two dunces together. "We've got to write a poem, and neither of us knows how to go about it!"

To which the servant replies, "But I do!"

As the two young gentlemen burst out laughing, he snatches from their hands the sheets of paper—as large as a newspaper page—and reads aloud what they have written. The poems are stupid. The audience bursts into laughter, for he has read them in a way that makes them sound even sillier than they are.

The servant picks up a brush. With strokes both vigorous (to express the intensity of his inspiration) and abrupt (to show its suddenness) he jots down a few lines on each sheet. Then he reads his masterpieces aloud. The two good-for-nothings rush up and hug him, particularly the one who already feels that his night in bed is a sure thing.

At this point the family makes its ceremonious entrance: the father with slow and noble steps, the mother weighed down with domestic cares, and the two daughters, including the one married to the student. Meanwhile the servant prudently withdraws.

The two students rush forward and with comic haste recite their poems at the same time. The father and mother nod their heads, each in his and her fashion, as if to say: "It's beautiful. That's what poetry should be!"

But the daughter who loves the servant, or is at least not insensitive to his love, steps forward and snatches the two sheets of paper. The handwriting is not that of her sister's husband, she can see that at a glance. And the hoax is exposed, with a wild display of gestures. The married daughter brandishes her fists under her husband's nose while her sister points to the guilty author of the poems, without anyone's quite knowing whether she is annoyed at the trickery or proud of such splendid talent.

The guilty one is dragged to the front of the stage. Like the good Sganarelle that he is, he first makes all the right gestures to indicate that he is ashamed of his effrontery and that he is already repentant. Then, without transition, he declares with a lordly gesture that he is indeed the author of the masterpieces.

Tumult. Wild pantomime of the parents. Intervention of the fair one, who, on the one hand, is trying to calm her family and, on the other, moves toward him whose talent, which has been revealed in such masterly fashion, has aroused her admiration. He, seeing her enthusiasm, does not hesitate. Calling upon the audience to witness his boldness, he brushes against the girl, who assumes an air of outrage for the benefit of her parents and one of delight for that of her suitor. And, though the play is far from ended, the spectators already know that the battle is three-quarters won and that the longed-for union of the poor boatman and the beautiful girl is only a matter of time.

I took advantage of a brief pause to glance about me. Everyone was beaming with delight. The craftiness of the suitor was fully appreciated, and each of his asides was greeted with thrills of pleasure by every last spectator. Yet the audience was a thoroughly popular one, and not, as in Western theaters, an audience of sophisticates. The force of the Chinese theater lies in the fact that it responds to a taste and need felt by everyone. All alike find delight in it because culture among them is not a prerogative of the few. It is everywhere. Every Chinese is a man of culture, and that perhaps is what distinguishes the Chinese from other peoples. A scholar had explained the matter to me as follows: "In the West, culture starts at the top and gradually seeps downward. It comes from without and ultimately, perhaps, works its way inward. Among us, the process is the reverse. It has its origin in each individual and spreads outward. Thus it is, if I may say so, centrifugal. It is not only an ethic which is subject to very strict and very ancient rules, but also an art of living that each individual cultivates for himself. To be sure, we have rich persons and poor. But you will find wisdom and philosophy in the street porter no less than in the rich merchant, with the result that there is a 'level' that exists nowhere else."

Another thing that makes the Chinese theater accessible to all is pantomime. We of the West have lost the art of the mime, but the Chinese continue to excel in it. How superior it is to language! Not only does it not restrict meaning, as do words, but it enables each individual spectator to interpret what he sees in his own way. (Is it not because of pantomime that Charlie Chaplin was so great, so universal, in the silent films? Are not the three minutes of gesturing by Jean-Louis Barrault in *Les Enfants du Paradis* worth more than the rest of the film?) Can you imagine a Western play with the qualities of

both *Macbeth* and *Punch and Judy?* Yet that is what I saw
before me. Children and adults were equally delighted.
They were fascinated not only by the splendor of the
costumes but also by the actors' pantomime, in which
one of the players rushed at the other and beat him
grandiloquently, while the other leaped about to show
his terror and the pain caused by the blows. Who among
us, young or old, does not love the magical, the marvelous? Who among us does not like to see a man baffled
and beaten? These are universal themes that everyone un-
derstands. That was why the children were also having
a wonderful time. And, like good Chinese, thoroughly
indulging their pleasure, they went right up to the foot-
lights in order to see better. And we who were in the first
row of the orchestra suddenly found ourselves behind a
triple row of youngsters who had wormed their way from
all parts of the theater through the legs of the adults and
were now stretching their necks to get a better view. And
the grownups were quite indulgent and did not in the least
mind. They were all completely relaxed, thoroughly at
ease. One man was leaning quite casually against his
neighbor in order to see better; another, a fat fellow,
stretched out his full length so that his belly might have
full latitude for laughter. Nobody minded such offhandedness, for the Chinese, despite his free and easy ways, is
never vulgar. . . . But to come back to the children: some
of them, craftier than the others, or perhaps more eager
to see the show, had slipped into the wings. And they
overflowed onto the stage, half naked as they were—and
some were even stark naked!

Toward midnight my friends decided to leave the
theater. The play was still going on. The atmosphere of

the house was thick with joy, sweat, and the smell of the hot fritters that were sold throughout the performance.

When the evening was over I found myself wondering why the Chinese had such a passion for the theater, for it is no common thing to see a street porter pay nine dollars to attend a performance of a classic.

The explanation of this phenomenon is, I think, that the theater in China is not only an entertainment but a source of information and an educational institution of prime importance. Through it the Chinese learns history, as we did in the past through the medieval mystery plays and verse chronicles. By means of the classical costumes and the nobility of the actors' style, the entire past unfolds before his eyes. He witnesses a parade of mandarins, emperors, princesses, concubines, and lackeys. He fills his eyes with an age that thereby is for him forever present. If he does not know history he learns it; if he does, then he reviews it. And not only does he see these typical characters working their way through a plot that thickens and unthickens with the subtlety dear to every Chinese, but he learns something that is even more universal, something that constitutes the foundation of his culture. He learns that every feeling is expressed by a form and that the quality of this form is intimately involved with that of content. It is to satisfy this innate love of form that he goes to the theater, a love that the theater also develops in him.

What is the origin of this love of form? And why are the Chinese, rich and poor alike, more artistic than any other people? Perhaps because they have always lived in a state of deep intimacy with Nature, who is the finest of artists, the most dazzling of craftsmen? Art, for

The Vietnamese street vendor . . .

and the Chinese . . .

the Chinese, is life itself as well as an integral part of everyday life. And he cultivates it even in the most trivial details of existence. Take the basketmaker and see what he manages to do with bamboo fiber. This fiber, the toughest yet most flexible of all, he slits into strands so fine that the baskets he weaves are veritable lacework! Yet these articles are intended for ordinary domestic use. But is it not in the most commonplace details that the spirit of a people is best revealed?

Take the street hawker pushing a packing box mounted on four tiny wooden wheels. It is only an old soapbox, but he has taken the trouble to paint it and adorn it with Chinese characters. On the case is a show window, and in this window is lettuce, and nothing else. Before setting out, the vendor sprinkled it with water. With the droplets gleaming beneath the glass, the green heads look like jade sculpture, rare jewels displayed in a case.

Or take another, who carries at either end of her pole —which imparts to her body the movements of a dancer —two trays filled with flowers. She has also set her flowers in two astonishingly light glass cases. Each case contains a central piece circled with a crown of little bright-colored pots, each containing two or three flowers. As the cages sway, the whole glimmers and takes on an enchanting quality. The casing not only protects the merchandise from dust but gives it an indefinable air of mystery and rarity. Merely to put three lemons under glass is to endow them with the value of treasure!

Take that withered-looking old man trotting along and bending under the weight of the burden he carries at either end of his pole. He is a simple fritter vendor; yet he too has his showcases. One contains fritters; the

77

other, square bottles full of various syrups, all glittering with colors. With the glistening of the surfaces, one side looks like a jeweler's window, the other like a display of perfumes.

On Sailors Street the lady who sells pet fish is sitting beside her jars, which are artfully arranged in tiers. Some of the jars are round and contain only a single rare fish. The others, which are rectangular, widen out at the mouth in order to give maximum visibility. The edges are beveled so as to catch the glints of the liquid. Not only are the fish themselves of astonishing form and color, but the vegetation amidst which they move is of such delicacy that one gets an impression of breathing rather than undulation. The customer makes his own choice. With a tiny spoon net he fishes out the creature and hands the net back to the vendor, who has been sitting motionless. She takes a water-lily leaf, folds it in the shape of a pocket, pours a little water, and places the fish in it. Then she lifts the edges of the leaf and knots them with a bit of raffia. The customer goes off carrying by the raffia string a fish that is comfortably cool. The wrapping has cost the vendor nothing yet is as functional as can be, for it is watertight and keeps the fish cool.

In all of this the presentation is so artful that the Chinese does not have to puff his goods. He is not a salesman who bawls his wares or buttonholes his customers. He has far too much dignity for that, and too much respect for others. In the shops you can browse about without the dealer's ever coming up to you. Never does he apply pressure. He does not even offer to help, leaving all salesmanship to his merchandise.

78

"*The fritter vendor too has his show cases. One contains fritters; the other, square bottles full of various sirups, all glittering with colors . . . Thus one side looks like a jeweler's window, the other like a display of perfumes.*"

"The fish jars . . . Some of them are round and contain only a single rare fish. The others are rectangular and widen out at the mouth in order to give the maximum visibility . . . And there is the water-lily leaf, folded up in the shape of a pocket, to allow the customer to carry off his choice . . ."

Take a certain restaurant on Jaccareo Street. Modest though it be, it is nevertheless placed under the triple sign of Fecundity, Wealth, and Honors, represented by a stag, a bat, and an old man, respectively. When the proprietor married off his daughter he felt the need to express this appeal for a threefold benediction even more vividly: by means of flowers. He engaged a group of floral craftsmen who, after assembling their creation in some blind alley, set it up over the restaurant, with friezes, cornices, and Chinese characters—fifteen inches high—all in flowers. To crown the work, they hooked on candelabra, likewise made of flowers. The candelabra were so elegant that they seemed rather to be a spray of precious stones set in rubies and diamonds. The spray itself was a marvelous expression of the vital impulse of the Chinese. Yet the work was meant to last only a few hours. As soon as the flowers wilted the display disappeared.

This enchantment of form is also to be found on the river. Look at those sampans, gliding over the water like certain insects whose bodies are composed of simple strokes and whose paws turn outward. The craft is operated by two men, one fore and one aft, who seem not so much to be rowing as doing a rhythmic dance step, for not only does the body counter like a stem but the outer leg draws back and forth with a ballet-like movement. Their oars are not rigid poles but long, supple reeds that, at the end of each stroke, whip the water like fins. Not only are they wonderfully functional, by virtue of that law whereby function creates form, but the form takes on meaning. The black-garbed boatmen, whose movements are so stylized, become hieratic figures. The junks

"*Look at those sampans, gliding over the water like insects . . .
Their oars are not rigid poles, but long, supple reeds that, at the
end of each stroke, whip the water like fins . . .*"

"*The craft is operated by men who seem not so much to be rowing as doing a rhythmic dance step, for not only does the body counter like a stem, but the outer leg draws back and forth with a ballet-like movement.*"

they maneuver become, by their form and the ritual objects adorning them, representatives of the Genius of the Waters.

Here is a last image. . . . It is one o'clock in the morning. The square beneath my balcony is dark and deserted. Suddenly the silence is broken by a melancholy clanging. A moment later a shadow emerges, that of a man on a tricycle. In the middle of the square he stops his vehicle. A small lamp goes on, needling the darkness with a red flower. Hardly has it started gleaming than five or six shadows surge up from nowhere and surround it, and all at once the night is peopled. But night in the Orient is never totally empty. The man has dismounted and removed a little stove from a drawer of his stall. In no time at all there is hot food, a lamp, and, above the lamp, a bouquet of flowers. An entire spectacle has risen up as if conjured from a hat like a rabbit or a lighted cigar.

By the time I had got a notebook to sketch the scene, the man had extinguished his stove and folded up his bag of tricks. All was still again.

"*The man has dismounted and removed a little stove from the drawer of his stall. In no time at all there is hot food, a lamp, and above the lamp a bouquet of flowers . . .*"

VIII

FROM the balcony of my room—every room of the hotel had its own balcony—I could see, on one side, Jaccareo Street and, on the other, the river.

Jaccareo Street is one of the most animated streets in Cholon. It is, on the one hand, Chinese, with its street stalls lined up at the edge of the sidewalk, its little restaurants that overflow onto the street, its artisans with their street stands, its itinerant peddlers, its opium den, which is wide open (the clients can be seen from the street lying on the flap beds), and the lively streets leading into it, and, on the other, international, because of the Rainbow, the most popular restaurant-dance-hall in town. The Rainbow is the center of attraction for Europeans. In the downstairs dining room, which is ventilated by twenty ceiling fans whose broad blades turn noiselessly, an army of Chinese waiters moves silently about the tables. There is something cool and iridescent about the establishment, and also something mysterious, something

dubious. The food is very fine and of the utmost variety.
The waiters are efficient. There is not merely one per
table, as in Europe, but three or four, not counting the
girl who, after each course, hands you, at the end of her
chopsticks, a hot, fragrant napkin so that you can freshen
up. Before long you begin to feel that all possibilities are
open to you. Would you care to have a private room?
You need only say the word. Musicians? Dancing girls?
You need only beckon. They are waiting for your sign.
The more desires you have, the more eager they will be
to satisfy them.

On the floor above is the night club, also a large room,
but of a rather mixed nature. The setting is European,
the orchestra Philippine, and the taxi girls, in their wonderfully form-fitting dresses, are Chinese. Their job is to
charm the client, but their seduction has nothing of the
"come-on" of Western "hostesses." Not only has their
attire a distinction that makes Western fashion pale into
insignificance, but they are also so reserved that whenever I had one of them at my table it was I who was
intimidated. They seemed not dance-hall girls but officiants performing a rite. The sight of them gliding along
the floor, with their eyes half closed and their faces lit
up as if from within, suggested idols of a pagoda.

This is enough to make visitors stream into the Rainbow and the streets to fill up, at the stroke of ten, with
elegant cars, the contrast of which with the poverty of
the crowd is sufficient to entertain the insatiable and
minute curiosity of the Chinese. The sidewalk opposite
the establishment becomes an observation post: for the
rubbernecks who observe intently every gesture of the
people going in; for the rickshaw boys, leaning on their

"In the past, it was a stone bridge, the approaches of which are still standing, with a stone stairway in Chinese Louis XV style, spreading out right and left. At present, it is a simple iron hog-backed gangway . . ."

vehicles, who scan the faces of the clients for the slightest sign; for all those who have something to offer, an opium pipe in a select place, a girl, or other more particular pleasures. For the Chinese, everything is "business." Nearby are several hotels, with their names in Chinese characters beaming like so many stars.

The other view from my window was that of a broad square at the other side of a bridge that spans the Arroyo. In the past it was a stone bridge, the approaches to which are still standing, with a stone stairway in Chinese Louis XV style, spreading out right and left. At present it is a simple iron hog-backed gangway. The people who move across it are, for a moment, picturesquely profiled against the sky before disappearing from sight beyond the midway point.

There is a constant flow of people across the bridge all day long, for the bridge separates two worlds, on this side the Chinese and on the other the Vietnam. Vietnam peddlers haul their wares to Jaccareo Street; water carriers, their bodies gleaming with sweat, climb the stairs sideways in order to reduce the effort; charwomen are recognized by the umbrellas they carry under their arms; cripples hobble along with the pathos of the Oriental; kids run between the legs of the grownups and are roundly scolded by those they collide with. The two-way stream of ants goes on and on until late in the night.

But most picturesque of all is the entrance to the bridge, which is flanked by a huge billboard advertising Martell's Cognac. The wall just below the billboard forms a big straight section and is a favorite stopping place. The rickshaw boys stand there in the shade, awaiting a possible client. The fritter and watermelon men

"*Water carriers, their bodies gleaming with sweat, who climb the stairs sideways in order to reduce the effort . . .*"

"On either side of the gangway and all along the embankment are warehouses containing rice and wood, and also some haughty mansions of great merchants."

take up their posts there because of the traffic that goes by the bridge. Women pause there to catch their breath before mounting the steep steps with their loads. It is also the spot chosen very shrewdly by the bicycle repairer. To judge from the vehicles all about him, the man does a thriving business. . . . People also stop to urinate against the wall, and without the slightest embarrassment, the women standing and the men squatting, quite the opposite of us. There too is where lovers meet and engage in long dialogues, in the shadow of Martell's Cognac. And, to complete the picture, that is where the sweepings of the square are heaped up. Despite the fact that it is removed from time to time, the pile quickly reappears. And the stench does not seem to disturb anyone.

On either side of the gangway and all along the embankment are warehouses containing rice and wood, and also some great merchants' haughty mansions. Huddled down below, on a level with the water—and even on the water, for most of them are set on piles—are thousands of straw huts, all of them more or less ramshackle and worm-eaten. In these live the men who work on the sampans and junks. They constitute a world apart and are utterly different in appearance from the inhabitants of the town. They have smooth dark hair and are fierce-looking. Their uniformly black outfit makes them look like outlaws. It is there that they live and die, by the shore of this river which is neither water nor earth, but a dark mass composed of mud, gleaming trickles of fuel oil, excrement, and other viscous matter; in dwellings that, as a result of age and droppings, cling to each other and form a single block. At times the tide, which goes up the fifty miles of river, raises the level of the sea milkwort so that their sampan houses float, and each passing steamer drives toward the bank a big black wave that makes the whole structure pitch; when the water recedes it leaves behind a veritable cesspool, a mass of filth in which the children wade waist-high.

But each hut, however poor, has its dedication to the gods (in the form of a pennant), its altar of the ancestors, and its incense sticks that burn day and night.[1] Here, somewhat apart from the other dwellings, is a decrepit-looking boat that probably has not sailed for years. Though it is only three feet wide and ten long, a whole family lives in it . . . and probably has been living in it for generations. Under the palm-leaf roof one can make out silhouettes. The woman is moving about busily. The man is lying on his back and smoking opium. The children are wading in the muck. With much squealing and yelling they dash forward to the middle of the river and cling in a bunch to the rudder of a passing barge in order to treat themselves to a joy ride.

There is also a pig in the boat, a coal-black suckling, no

---

[1] It may interest the reader to know how these sticks are made. Three quarters of the stick is composed of wood dust, which is obtained by grinding wood in stone mortars with primitive pestles. The other quarter is a compressed substance composed of the bark of elm root reduced to powder and thinned with water, to which is added scented powders thinned in Chinese wine (the usual scents are incense, clove, camphor, and certain odoriferous woods such as cyprus). These powders are all ground together and made into a binding paste which is placed in a kind of pump. The mass is then crushed energetically and emerges, molded like thick wire, from round holes at the end of the apparatus. All that remains is to dry the pasty sticks and cut them up into the ritual lengths, generally six or seven inches. The sticks are then sold in batches of 19, 37, 61, and 91.

"Somewhat apart from the others is a decrepit-looking boat that probably hasn't sailed for years. Though it is only three feet wide and ten long, a whole family lives in it . . . and probably has been living in it for generations . . ."

doubt the family's finest possession, for though the children are skinny the animal is plump.

On the roof of the sampan is a small tray with the ritual bowl of incense, and zinnias in a blue pot. Is it happiness or misery that is to be found on this boat that looks like a tiny Noah's Ark aground on the strand of the ages?

With the coming of evening, the two shores of the Arroyo present a striking contrast. Here, the hum of movement, the twinkling of a thousand lights; there, silence and darkness, dotted with an occasional flicker. Between them, on the river, lights move about like will-o'-the-wisps. They are the boat lanterns. Each boat has its own, hanging from the end of a pole. But they look rather like lost spirits wandering about aimlessly.

One evening as I was walking back to my hotel I heard unwonted musical sounds coming from the boulevard—not the nasal twanging of Chinese music that phonographs grind out but something that sounded like sobs.

I went to see what it was about and found myself in the middle of a crowd of people gathered around two musicians, each sitting on a small folding chair. One was playing a sixteen-string zither that he held on his knees. He was hitting the strings with two little hammers, the bamboo heads of which were so supple and elastic that they rebounded with the shock, thereby enabling the musician to perform with incredible rapidity. The second musician was the violinist, though it was difficult to tell which of the two was accompanying the other. He was playing a Chinese violin, the body of which was a gourd, over which was stretched a skin. From the middle emerged a long neck with two strings tightened at the top by two long pear-shaped wooden pegs. With one hand the man held the neck at the middle, but he did not pinch the strings. He simply pressed them against the neck with more or less force, while holding the instrument so that it was not vertical but turned outward. With the other hand he manipulated the bow, the arm being curved upward. But the bow, instead of moving along the upper surface of the cords, as with our violins, was set between the two strings of the instrument. This technique produced a hollow note, a plaintive wail that seemed to emerge from the night.

There was no score. With their eyes half closed as if in a trance, the two musicians played endless variations on the same theme, without even consulting each other. They merely paused from time to time, not, so it seemed, to catch their breath, but rather to draw fresh inspiration from within themselves. Then the zitherist began again with renewed vigor, somewhat as an insect resumes its flight.

The bystanders were very grave, as if some secret aspect of their inner nature were being revealed to them. The instruments that were being played dated from remote antiquity, and I had the impression that, thanks to them, I was moving back into the night of time.

Though the Chinese of Cholon have admitted jazz to their night clubs as a concession to their foreign clientele, nevertheless, for their own pleasure, they remain devoted to their traditional music of "silk and bamboo," as it is called. (Silk is for stringed instruments and bamboo for wind instruments.) Thus one finds in Cholon all the instruments used in ancient China, instruments with names

97

as strange as their shapes: the mouth flute, the transverse flute or "mouth organ," "the butterfly harp," "the moon guitar." These instruments are far superior to modern ones in rendering the infinite nuances of the Chinese soul.

In regard to tools as well, the people of Cholon stick to their old forms, for example, hieratic scissors, lobed planes, brooms in the form of peacocks' tails, fans of paper or bustard feathers with horned handles. And they manage to Chinify even modern objects. They can take a slat framework with hooks attached, suspend within it a couple of lacquered ducks, surmount it with a paper lantern, and thus turn it into a Chinese showcase. In like manner they thoroughly orientalize their trucks, which are probably bought from army surplus stock: the body is painted bright green and decorated with large red Chinese characters. The machine looks all the more exotic as it is covered with a roof of palm sticks held together by bamboo fiber. Add to this a chauffeur stripped to the waist, who drives barefoot, and, inside, under the roof, a few coolies, also half naked, and you have the mystery and the almost disquieting quality that China has for the Westerner.

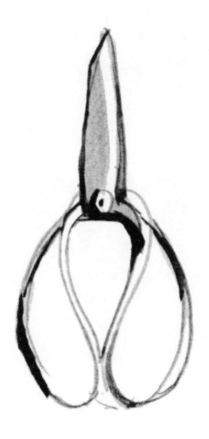

"In regard to tools as well, the people of Cholon stick to their old forms, for example hieratic scissors . . ."

"*In like manner, they thoroughly orientalize their trucks, which are probably bought from army surplus stocks; the body is painted bright green and decorated with large red Chinese characters. The machine looks all the more exotic as it is covered with a roof of palm sticks, held together by bamboo fibre . . .*"

IX

If I use the word "disquieting," I do so because, despite everything, I always had an uneasy feeling whenever I moved among the Chinese crowd. Each of my walks— the best I could do, being unable to speak the language, was to stroll about the streets—was a strange anthropological excursion, so much so that I would often wonder whether the people I saw about were not of a species totally different from ours.

Here is a creature moving slowly amidst the crowd. It looks rather like an old cayman; its inert expression is that of a cayman warming itself in the sun, particularly as its open mouth reveals saurian teeth. There is not the slightest quiver of expression in its vacant gaze.

Here is another, a street porter who has laid his load of wood on the sidewalk and is scratching himself in the sun. The skin of his body is as shiny and puckered as that of an old iguana.

Take that truck driver who, while waiting for the un-

"Take that truck driver . . . Wi[th?]
his slits of eyes (impossible to s[ee?]
their gaze) the terrifying bone stru[c-]
ture of his face and his upper lip th[at]
juts out over a broad mouth [in]
which two large teeth are gleamin[g,]
he looks like a hangman, the cr[uel]
Chinese torturer of legend, with [the]
impassivity that belongs [to]
Mongols."

loading to begin, has just planted himself in front of me on the sidewalk. With his slits of eyes (impossible to see their gaze), the terrifying bone structure of his face, and his upper lip that juts out over a broad mouth in which two large teeth are gleaming, he looks like a hangman, the cruel Chinese torturer of legend, with the impassivity that belongs to Mongols. His arms are crossed over his stout muscles. His torso is too long for his short legs, and his reddish body looks as though he had bathed in blood. He is barefoot and wears only a pair of blue-striped shorts held up by a cord. On his head is an old felt hat of which he has trimmed away half the brim, and this Western headgear, warped and battered and too narrow for his skull, produces a very striking effect. The man has been standing there for quite a while, facing the crowd, with an inscrutable expression. All at once he turns about and sets to work with astonishing speed.

What human species are they? There was something astonishing in the bony structure of almost every individual I saw before me. They seemed to be the work of a moonstruck Rodin, of an artist who had taken hold of a normal mask, battered it in with his fist, and then, picking up a chisel, dug deep grooves in order to set off the bones, the zygomatic holes.

It is not only that many of them are lean but the fact that this leanness often assumes strange forms. There is the fleshlessness of the necks, which are veritable turtle or lizard necks. There is the Adam's apple that protrudes like an egg—when it doesn't hang out; the pointed shoulder blades, projecting at the lower base like those of monkeys. They also have the long fingers of monkeys, stuck together and set opposite the thumb.

As for the fat Chinese, they look like moonfish, and their short arms resemble fins. Some of them have such folds of fat on their bellies that as they move forward they suggest walruses propelling themselves through the water. Sometimes I would see lemurians, or, considering their froglike eyelids, batrachians.

What struck me above all was the fact that the faces of individuals did not reflect their inner nature. How can we convince ourselves that a totally expressionless saurian mask hides the keenest intelligence, or that what looks like a pithecanthropus is endowed with extreme artistic sensibility? Despite my efforts to understand, these two phenomena remain irreconcilable. I am not the first to wonder at this, for upon my return I came across the following in Kayserling's *Travel Journal:* "I begin to understand why Europeans so readily look upon the Chinese as monsters of a sort. Anyone who compares them to monkeys should reflect upon what constitutes the grotesqueness of the monkeys. It lies in the contrast between an eye gleaming with human intelligence and an animal face. Hence, any eye that is extremely intelligent and at the same time very alive gives to the physiognomy a certain simian quality."

There is something disturbing in this. But may not the explanation lie in the fact that the Chinese, from the earliest ages, has lived close to Nature and has remained part of her? He has never ceased to be a man of the earth, living as close as possible to Nature, feeling himself part of her and identifying himself with her in all his acts, like our own men of the soil. Has their physical type evolved? No more, apparently, than have the forms of Nature been modified! Nature is stability. She resists evolution

"What human species are they? There was something astonishing in the bone structure of almost every individual that I saw before me. They seemed to be the work of a moon-struck Rodin . . ."

"It is not only that many of them are lean, but the fact that this leanness assumes strange forms . . ."

"There is the fleshlessness of the necks, which are veritable turtle or lizard necks. There is the Adam's apple that protrudes like an egg, when it doesn't hang out . . ."

"As for the fat Chinese . . . some of them have such folds of fat on their bellies that they suggest walruses propelling themselves through the water . . ."

and opposes the development of the individual as such, because she is grounded in the generic and individual development is contrary to the generic. Among us, the man
of the soil is more of a type than an individual; he is a
Breton or Auvergnat type, as a tree is an oak or elm
type. And the truer the oak runs to type the better
it conserves its intrinsic qualities. I know peasants who
are of the mole type; their gestures are far closer to those
of the mole than of the intellectual. But they are nonetheless clever farmers precisely because they "belong" to
the soil and have deep and subtle affinities with it.
Moreover, their work requires such communion, and
this understanding is at the opposite pole from the com-
prehension of the intellect, which, by its abstractness, departs from nature. The man of the earth abstracts
nothing; he concretizes everything. He will speak of
autumn weather with low-lying clouds as "old weather"
and will say of a sick man that "it's the fever that's driv-
ing him"—and we see the sufferer being swept along by
his fever at a mad pace. Thus he poetizes in all
naturalness.

I know an old man in my native village, so hairy a
fellow that the children grow frightened when he appears
on the square. He sleeps in the woods "so as to be closer
to things," and he spurns soap because "it's bad for the
skin," leaving it to the morning dew to "scour his eyes."
Some of the villagers call him "Lousy-beard," derisively,
but I have nicknamed him "Golden-beard" because his
beard, the color of which varies with the seasons, turns
russet in the autumn like a burning bush and, when the
sun is on it, is spangled with flakes of light. He has an

almost divinatory knowledge of life and animals, and when he speaks of them he has a language of his own that seems to rise from some mysterious source.

I also know a river poacher, a man who is in such intimate communion with his river that his body senses its slightest changes of mood. At any given moment he can tell you where the fish are keeping themselves. He too looks like a primitive, with mustaches that suggest the wattles of a fish, and perhaps they serve as antennae, for his communion with the water and the elements are of a peculiar intimacy, a blend of respect and fervor.

It rather seems that something of the same sort exists among the Chinese and that they are moved by form as my local primitives are moved by the upward thrust of the tree trunk or the bend of the river, though with this difference: that for the Chinese there is no sentiment. For him, form is self-sufficient and needs no adjunct of romanticism. Form in itself is sufficient to exalt him, as three apples in a dish exalted Cézanne. He sees through form to essence and, like the surrealist, he seeks to "represent inner reality and outer reality as two elements in the process of unification." Is not the spirit of things expressed in nature by forms and colors? Serenity is expressed by the tranquil face of a lake, tumult by the bubbling of the waters of a river. Is not form sufficient to reveal the inner quality of things? Does not the bark of the oak best express solidity and strength, and the undulation of seaweed suppleness and grace? These things render the essence of being more completely than does language, and in a more varied way, for Nature offers in her forms a thousand types of force and fragility.

Thus, in his writing, the Chinese has tried to represent, graphically and symbolically, every feeling by a form, and to express its various shades by forms.

Take, for example, the idea of "anger." It can be a whirlwind; in which case it will be rendered by a whirling form. It can be a cry; the form will then be a mouth, wide open and screaming. It can be animosity; it will be rendered by an image of two individuals affronting each other. If it is meanness, it will be presented in the form of a fire-spitting hydra. A threat? It becomes a raised ax or an arm about to strike. Venomous? It will be a snake with a hissing tongue. Fearful? Something twisted. Sullen? A rumbling volcano. It can also have a color or a sound.

Thus the Chinese will not only have expressed the idea of anger but will have described its exact shade, or its color. How much more precise this is than language!

Likewise in the theater. I have spoken, in describing the scene of the two students at grips with their assignment, of *boredom*. How many variants of boredom the Chinese actor can express! How broad the range of his pantomime! Is the boredom a matter of mere fretting? The actor sucks his brush in the hope of extracting ideas from it, or he nibbles at his nails. Does inspiration refuse to come? He rubs his head vigorously. Is the problem gnawing at him? He scratches his chest. Is boredom paralyzing him? He shakes his lower limbs to fight against the invading numbness. Is the boredom oppressive? He lets his head fall backward, or else collapses on the table. Is his sight growing dim? He rubs his eyes vigorously to dissipate the blur. Each nuance is so sharply defined that the spectators cannot fail to grasp it, and so suggestive that each person can incorporate it and make it his own.

But let us go back to my hotel; it is not only a spectacle but also, for the Westerner, a school of apprenticeship. Do you have difficulty putting up with noise? Do you like to be alone occasionally? Do you go to bed early and do you need peace and quiet in order to rest? If so, go and live for a while in a Chinese hotel. I know no better therapy. And it will act upon you twenty hours a day with an insistence and persuasiveness that are irresistible. In order that no one in the hotel may miss anything of what goes on there, not only must your door remain open, but all the compartments communicate with each other by means of an openwork grating at the top of each wall, which makes possible, at all hours, communication, if not by sight, at least by hearing and smell. Without stirring from the couch where you have stretched out, you are, whether you like it or not, "in" on all the activities of the house. You accompany on his strolls the guest in Room 24 whose shuffle you have learned to recognize. Despite yourself, you follow the bookkeeper in his calculations by the clicking of his abacus. You also take part in the game of mahjong going on down the hall, and the clicking of the tiles and the noisy shuffling that follows will tell you exactly what pitch the game has reached. You will be a party—eight compartments away —to the quarrel that breaks out every evening between a *Fat Lan Sai* (a Frenchman) and the Chinese lady with whom he lives secretly, that is, as far as the rest of the world is concerned, for we of the hotel do not miss a single detail of their domestic strife. Through the smothered laughter of the boys and the violent tone that the Cantonese sometimes assume among themselves, you will find yourself involved in their discussions, just as you will be pecked at by the rapid chatter of the boyesses sitting together in the corridor, on benches, in groups of three and four.

And at night neither the activity nor the noise abates. At whatever hour I returned home, something was always going on. I recall one of the boys at the hotel who, having bought a Chinese violin, was learning to play with a handbook before him, and the entire floor staff zealously helped him to interpret the instructions. Another boy, in a fit of emulation, had got hold of a zither (the effect was that of a cat being slowly flayed and refusing to die). After two hours of such practicing, the boys dropped their instruments and attacked the phonograph. This produced more caterwauling, even worse than what had preceded it because the volume was turned on full blast, as always. There everyone was free. Had I liked, I would have been free to play the "Marseillaise," while another phonograph farther off roared out a nasal "Auld Lang Syne" in a Chinese adaptation.

And while all this goes on, there rise up to you from the street—and bear in mind that the windows have no panes—the tinkling of the street vendors' bells, the piercing clang-clang of the rickshaws, and the intermittent braying of a showboat going up the river.

Toward 1 A.M. things seem to calm down. The boys set up their camp beds in the lobby. But apparently they still have things to say to each other, for they start chattering in bed, with "ha-hahs" and "ho-hos" that leave no doubt as to their high spirits. And you who are desperately trying to fall asleep mutter, "Another five minutes of this and I'll raise a riot!" But you'd better not. You would only be regarded as an ill-tempered *sai yan,* and you would pay for your indiscretion later. The mere fact of having gone through the lobby one day with a frown brought me a week of reprisals. And the Chinese have a way of suddenly ceasing to understand your requests.

Finally, one after the other, the boys drop off to sleep, but then the snoring starts, and if you have never heard a Chinese snore you have no idea of what snoring can be. It's neolithic.

Meanwhile, in your room, the gray lizards give vent to their tsik-tsik-tsik. As long as the light is on they keep chasing mosquitoes. And you cannot ignore their chase, which is all the more fascinating to follow in that they approach by a series of bounds. When the insect has been snapped up they clean their eyes . . . with their tongues. If you put out the light the hunting stops and their amorous play begins. At last you fall asleep, exhausted by all these nocturnal activities, when suddenly a frightful caterwauling breaks out on the roof. One of the hotel toms has got hold of a female. For three days he had been planning the job but, like a good Chinese, he had probably waited for a "lawful" day, according to the Calendar of Rites.

X

NEVER would I have thought, before living among the Chinese, that the lives of six hundred million human beings could be regulated, to the minutest details, by a kind of farmer's almanac. Yet such was the case, for the Chinese is a son of nature and, as such, subject to the seasons to the lunar variations, to all the tellurian and cosmic influences. He knows, as do our own peasants, who have the kind of knowledge for which no book learning can ever substitute, that all things in nature hang together, and, as Lao-tse said, that "all is in one, one is in all." His entire universe, not only the physical but the moral and social universe, is founded on this concept. For him, the universe is an integral whole, wonderfully balanced yet at the same time fragile because the equilibrium can be upset by the merest trifle, and the slightest disturbance can set off a chain reaction, the consequences of which are unforeseeable. Hence the extreme prudence with which he performs every act. In like manner the invisible world is, to him, merely the extension of the visible world to which it is closely linked. The "Empire Above" is both architecturally and socially an exact replica of the "Empire Below," with its High Officials— that is how the Chinese conceive the celestial divinities— surrounded by Assessors who in turn supervise other functionaries of lesser importance. These "celestial functionaries" must be honored according to their rank, and should be invoked at the most favorable time (as indicated in the Calendar of Rites), to the accompaniment of offerings. The value of these depends on the official you wish to "reach" and must be of a kind likely to prompt the said official to direct his benevolence to you —if he is a functionary benevolent by nature—or, in the case of a malevolent official, to soften him, for with the Chinese there is always a way out.

In all these transactions the supreme guide is the Calendar of Rites, which is on sale everywhere. This calendar regulates Chinese life down to the most minor act and indicates in each case the precautions to be taken. It also indicates the days which are "lawful" for performing such and such an act and "unlawful" for such and such another; failure to observe these prescriptions entails the most serious danger. And not only for the days but for the hours. Today, at a given hour, you may sweep your house, but you may not conclude a business deal or have a suit cut.

This Chinese concept does not date from yesterday, for the first notation of the universe by simple symbols goes back to the reign of the Emperor Fu Hsi, around 2800 B.C.

These notations derive from the fundamental idea that

there are two basic elements in the world, the Yang, which is the positive and male principle, and the Yin, the negative and female principle, which are found everywhere. The Yang represents the sun as opposed to the moon, light as opposed to darkness, hot to cold, south to north, dry to damp, and many other pairings, all dominated by the idea of rhythm, of fluctuation. "The Yang calls, the Yin replies." There is the opposition of the sexes, then their fusion, creating a rhythmic movement, forward and backward. It is also the alternate triumph of now one, now the other. In winter the Yang withdraws into the depths and the Yin dominates: there is dampness, darkness, and cold. In the spring the Yang re-emerges and bursts forth; it is the torrent that flows after the melting of the snow, it is the rising wheat. Males and females then begin their play, forming two rival yet interdependent groups. They interpenetrate and, according to the Hi Tseu, mingle their "sexual liquors." This is an endless movement, a quasi-ritual harmony, a nature dance become liturgical. All Chinese writings exalt the play of the Yang and the Yin.[1]

Starting from these two elements, the former of which is represented by a long unbroken line and the latter by two short lines, the Chinese established, in the reign of Fu Hsi, their first notation of the universe. They took eight basic elements:

Heaven ━━━━━━━   River ━━ ━━
       ━━━━━━━   ━━━━━━━
       ━━━━━━━   ━━━━━━━

[1] See Marcel Granet, *Chinese Thought.*

Earth ⚏ Mountain ⚎

Water ☵ Wind ☴

Fire ☲ Thunder ☳

These eight elements are grouped about the universe, which is represented by a circle, not cut in two but divided so that each half is in the form of a drop and the two halves penetrate each other in undulatory and "spermatic" fashion.

According to the Chinese *Book of Mutations*—the *Pa Kua*—these eight elements can, by association, form sixty-four possible combinations. Thus we have an entire philosophical system.

Another system of decomposing the world is based on numbers, which have a particular fascination for the Chinese. Starting with the number five, the system distinguishes five elements, five activities, five tastes and five musical notes. Below is the table of correspondences:

GEOGRAPHICAL POINTS	SEASONS	ELEMENTS	TASTES	MUSICAL NOTES
North	Winter	Water	Salty	Fourth Note
South	Summer	Fire	Bitter	Second Note
East	Spring	Wood	Acid	Fifth Note
West	Autumn	Metal	Tart	Third Note
Center	Center	Earth	Sweet	First Note

The developments are infinite. Likewise the systems. I should like simply to note the fact that the Chinese calendar is a double one composed of the lunar calendar with "big months" of thirty days and "small months" of twenty-nine days, and the solar calendar; and there is a complicated system whereby the two are adjusted to each other. As for the years, they follow a duodecimal cycle called "Terrestrial Branches"; each year corresponds to an animal:

> 1955 is the year of the sheep
> 1956 is the year of the monkey
> 1957 is the year of the cock

> 1958 is the year of the dog
> 1959 is the year of the pig
> 1960 is the year of the rat
> 1961 is the year of the ox
> 1962 is the year of the tiger
> 1963 is the year of the hare
> 1964 is the year of the dragon
> 1965 is the year of the snake
> 1966 is the year of the horse.

Whereupon the cycle starts again. But beware! For the:

> horse has an aversion to the ox
> rat has an aversion to the sheep
> dog has an aversion to the cock
> hare has an aversion to the dragon
> snake has an aversion to the tiger
> pig has an aversion to the monkey.

It would therefore be highly imprudent for a girl born under the sign of the horse to marry a man born under the sign of the ox, and so on.

Chinese mythology and the beliefs it engenders and rites it requires are a labyrinth. Here is a brief survey based on the voluminous study of Father Doré.[2]

Inventory of a Chinese House

In front of the house, at a certain distance, is erected a small wall of honor, on which is generally inscribed the character FU, meaning happiness.

Frequently the main door of the house is oriented obliquely to prevent the evil spirits from entering, for the

---

[2] *Superstitions in China,* 17 volumes.

Chinese believe that the spirits move only in a straight line.

On each side of the door are two ornamental stones called "projecting stones." They usually contain the following emblems: three arrows against demons, the two characters signifying wealth and nobility, a crane (bird of longevity), two horses adorned with gold and silver ingots (of paper), and a unicorn carrying a child.

Beside the door is a niche, three feet high, in which is a statue of the Agent of Heaven *(T'ien Koan)*.

Above the door is a scroll containing the "longevity" character between two peonies (symbol of wealth), the eight emblems (flute, saber, fan, basket of peaches, fly swatter, gourd, lotus flower, and phoenix feather) of the Eight Occult Immortals, the two principles, Yang and Yin, and the eight trigrams.

Above the window is the head of a wild beast to frighten away the evil spirits that might try to enter through it.

On the roof of the house is a genie in a niche, the "Marshal of the Tiles."

Under a beam of the roof: two sapeks for insuring wealth.

Under a flagstone: two knives to ward off brigands.

Hanging from the ceiling: a piece of wood attached by a string to avoid anyone's hanging himself in the house.

In a hole: seven nails tied together to insure the union of the members of the household.

In the first room, opposite the entrance door, is a large image, the Tchong T'ang, occupying the place of honor. It represents the divinities who are held in particular veneration by the inhabitants of the place (God of War for military men, of Letters for men of learning, of Wealth for the others). Beside this image is the ancestors' shelf, containing a perfume brazier in which there is always incense burning.

Hanging from the beams: various talismans, depending on the day and season. Thus, on the eve of the Chinese New Year, an image of the God of the Hearth is pasted on the stove. Then, with great pomp, everyone goes to welcome him upon his return from heaven where he is supposed to go once a year to make his report on the inhabitants of the dwelling.

Thus the life of a Chinese unfolds with an incredible wealth of precaution from before his birth until after his death. Scarcely is the mother pregnant before the family starts soliciting the protection and favor of the divinities. And the divinities are innumerable. Here it is the Taoist goddess, surrounded by her acolytes, one of whom governs fecundity, the second confinement, and the third posterity. Elsewhere people pray to the Holy Mother, Queen of Heaven, T'ien Heu Tcheng Mou, or to the famous Koan Yang Pou-sah, whose image is in all the pagodas. In the case of a mandarin family, the members invoke Koei-sing, the God of Literature, or Liu Tong Pong, the "Immortal of the Scholars," in order to have an intelligent child. If the confinement is a difficult one, the shelf of the Goddess of Delivery is carried to the home in great pomp. Or else the bonzes make amulets, talismans that need simply be pasted to the woman's body for the delivery to take place.

. As soon as the child is born the family calls in diviners to cast his horoscope and to know the "customhouses"

124

that he will have to go through until the age of sixteen (the list of these customhouses fills two pages). The child must also wear during his early years: earrings "heavy enough so that the spirits cannot carry the child off"; a ring in his nose to "chain him to life" (or else a silver ring about his neck, the key of which is kept by the bonze); a jade seal, "sovereign against fear"; a tiger's claw, "sovereign against enemies"; sapeks strung on a red cord and worn about the neck "to insure wealth"; a red dot on the cheeks, "sign of happiness and life"; a clasp of the "hundred families," a collective gift from the neighbors. Certain talismans contain tantrist formulas against sickness. And a thouand other precautions must be taken as the child grows up. You must not rejoice too much in the fact that he is well grown lest you arouse the jealousy of the gods. You must give the child the name of an animal ("Kitten" or "Puppy"). In that way the spirits will think he is not a human being and will not molest him. Or else you must give him a girl's name so as to mislead the spirits, who, as everyone knows, are concerned only with males. In any case you must not give him a definite name before puberty.

In regard to betrothal and marriage, the following gives some idea of the rites. To begin with, a go-between is instructed to make the first advances. If all goes well, the two families then exchange "eight-character notes," which provide full information about the future bride and bridegroom. These notes are carefully examined by the diviners, who compare them to see whether there is a likelihood of harmony. This is followed by the suitor's sending of the first gifts. If nothing unpleasant follows, the marriage day, approved by the diviners, is officially registered in red (the color of happiness). Then there is the exchange, definitive this time, of gifts, followed by the sending of the trousseau.

As for the marriage ceremony itself, which must always take place during the waxing of the moon, it is carried out in two stages. The first occurs at the bride's home and consecrates the breaking of the bonds uniting her with her parents. This severance is followed by a feigned kidnaping, conducted by the relatives and friends of the bridegroom who lead the girl to the home of her future husband. There the marriage is consecrated in the entrance hall. The girl, without her parents, who do not belong in a stranger's house, is wearing a red veil that hides her face and is carrying a red silk sachet embroidered with lotus flowers (in order to protect her against the possible maledictions of her mother-in-law). She and the groom prostrate themselves first before the shelves of the ancestors, then before the genie of the hearth and finally before the living parents, as a sign of submission. Having done this, they bow to each other gravely. The marriage is now ritually consecrated. The bride, whose husband is not supposed ever to have seen her face, then removes her veil. Everyone watches the reaction of the young couple, who are supposed to remain impassive (it would be dangerous to give vent to one's joy). Then comes a curious rite in which the new wife sits on the bed in the nuptial chamber (called the "Chamber of Joy") and is exposed to the coarse remarks of all those present. She must not laugh too much, for that would prove that she knows more than she is supposed to; nor must she get angry, for if she does she will lose face. After that, the guests, who have laughed abundantly and eaten copiously, withdraw. A few days later the bride pays the ritual visit to her parents in order "to be pardoned for the kidnaping."

Late one evening, as I was passing through one of the streets that lead into Jaccareo Street, I noticed on either side of a low door two large black and white Chinese lanterns, emblems of death, and, pasted to the wall of the house, a paper on which was inscribed the name of the dead person. Before the door stood a good-sized group, while strange music emerged from inside. I drew close, though somewhat hesitantly, for I thought that the presence of a *Sai Yan* might be unwelcome. But nobody seemed to pay any attention to me. As I learned later, anyone may join a funeral procession, on condition that he display the proper deference, and may take part in the rites of a pagoda even if he is not one of the faithful. How different this is from the practice in India, where in order to witness, inside a temple, the voluntary tortures that the faithful inflicted upon themselves I had had to place myself under the protection of a Brahmin, lest one of the fanatics take umbrage at my mere presence and stir up the crowd, in which case I would have been torn to pieces in an instant.

Here it was utterly different. Nor was it like the vigil in the West Indies, which is an occasion for rejoicing as well as lamentation, at which people drink hard in order to raise their spirits, and the mourners, aided by their natural buoyancy, play hide and seek around the corpse.

Here there was no gaiety. But the atmosphere was not painful, as among us, with some persons sobbing and others simulating grief. In such moments of trial the Chinese is more realistic and also more discreet. When he informs you of the death of a kinsman he does so with a smile. That does not mean he is joyful but simply that he does not want to "infect" you with his sorrow. The sorrow was not visible here. The tone was an odd mixture of impassiveness and ritual. The Chinese is not religious in our sense of the word. His religion is entirely a matter of respect for an order that has been established for thousands of years, and of prudence in regard to the mysterious forces of the life beyond. Regardless of whether he believes in their efficacy, he nevertheless observes the prescribed rites scrupulously, just as a European peasant goes to mass because "it can't do any harm." Even if intercession has no effect, it is better to follow the path of prudence. One never knows what may happen. Moreover, is it not a historical fact that the Chinese world, thus governed, has maintained itself more intact than any other? It has had a permanence that induces the individual to continue in the "way" of his ancestors. Therein, for him, lies eternity, in a present that is a constant link with the past—through the cult of ancestors who, from their shelf, watch over the daily lives of the living—and that is a guarantee of the future insofar as he maintains, in each of his acts, the order thus established.

In the entrance hall, at the right, lay the corpse in its bier. I had no idea how long it had been lying there waiting for the "lawful" day of burial. But I imagined, from the books I had read, the precautions and rites that had accompanied the dying. Even before the man was dead he had been taken from his bed, lest it be haunted later by his ghost, and made to lie elsewhere, without a pillow, so that he might die in peace (*p'ing* means both "peace" and "flat"; all of Chinese life is made up of such double meanings). He had been dressed in fine clothes for his journey to the other world. (The garments must be without buttons "so that the soul does not get hooked as it departs." They must not be woven with animal hair, lest the dead person run the risk of being reincarnated in the body of an animal.) Then someone walked around the house calling the dead man so as to be sure that his soul had unloosed itself. After that, the soul was led to the pagoda and delivered to the "celestial policeman" who had jurisdiction over the territory in which the man had died so that he would guard it for the time being.

The dead man was lying beneath a richly embroidered catafalque on which were several emblems, including that of the dragon and the "longevity" sign, for death does not break the chain. The dead man continues to depend on the living, who insure his survival, and in return the latter expect that he will shower them with blessings and prosperity.

Against the coffin was propped an enlarged color photograph of the deceased. At the foot of the coffin burned an oil wick, the "lamp of the days," which would continue to burn as long as the corpse was exhibited (in the past the period of exhibition was forty-nine days). The traditional sticks of incense were also burning in a bronze receptacle. All about were little heaps of ashes. These are kept and, on the eve of the burial, are sprinkled along the way that the dead man will follow.

Opposite the coffin, on the left side of the room, was a small table around which sat two bonzes, apparently Taoists, judging from the square skullcap each was wearing. They were reciting a kind of litany in a monotonous tone and, at regular intervals, struck a gong. This was the ceremony of the *pan-su* ("helping to pass the night"), which takes place late in the evening, usually on the third day after death. Two large red candles on the table added a touch of exorcism to the entire scene, while in the next room invisible musicians played the Chinese flute, which sounds like a bagpipe.

All about the bonzes, and even in the street, were the friends and relatives. The latter were all wearing, over their ordinary clothes, a kind of white harness (white being the color of mourning in China) which was tied at the waist and at the top of which was a hood that covered half the face. The relatives were standing about quietly, while the friends chatted in low voices about familiar matters.

A little way down the same street were two other lanterns, likewise indicating the presence of a corpse. Probably the family was of a different persuasion, for the officiants were not bonzes but five priestesses, all wearing the customary bluish-gray gown. They were reciting prayers with the utmost solemnity. From time to time one of them who seemed to be the chief officiant would strike a small gong in front of her. Whereupon the others would thrust their torsos forward. Then the chief officiant would raise a red stick that she held in her hand to the height of her face and, with clasped hands, make the gesture of the offertory, repeatedly bowing her head and raising her hands up and down. Sitting on the doorstep was a female flutist, dressed entirely in black, who joined in the rite sporadically, while another woman, squatting in front of her, fanned her with a purple fan.

In the back room invisible cymbalists accompanied the flute. At the flute player's feet was a white candle.

Three doors away was another corpse. There too the family was awaiting the lawful day of burial. In this house there was neither recitative nor music, probably because it was not the right day. The women simply sat in a circle on the floor in a state of solemn immobility.

The second day thereafter must have been the lawful day, for an endless stream of funeral processions flowed across the square under my balcony. The neighborhood dead were on their way to the cemetery. None of the processions that I saw had the amplitude or sumptuousness of certain funerals of earlier days, some of which would block all traffic for hours and hours. However, the ceremonies persisted. The families had probably observed the ritual precaution of lighting, on the eve of the funeral, small oil torches along the way that the procession was to pass. This is done to satiate the evil spirits . . . who love to lap up the oil!

The following is the composition of the procession, which wound through the crowd like a ribbon:

At the head of it was a man carrying, at the end of a long pike, a lighted lantern—this in broad daylight—in order to "light the way" for the soul of the defunct.

Behind him was a young boy carrying a banner on which the name and titles of the departed were inscribed in large characters. Strapped to the boy's back was a small drum which was struck at regular intervals by a man behind him. This is done to "let the spirits know that the dead man is going by."

Then came musicians, each wearing a long brownish-red smock and a broad-rimmed hat shaped like a flat cake and surmounted with a pointed crown. They were playing flutes and other nasal-toned instruments. The Chinese funeral being a festival, it is fitting to make a great deal of noise, and also to cheer up the dead man.

Behind them, as a kind of reliquary, came a sedan chair containing a photograph of the deceased and the clothes he would need in the world beyond—or rather artfully made paper clothes, for the Chinese realized ages ago that they could replace the real thing by an imitation without the gods being any the wiser. The sedan is supposed to "convey the soul to the nether regions." After the interment it is burned, for it is in danger of being haunted. The clothes and all paper objects accompanying the deceased are also burned in accordance with the deep-seated belief of the Chinese that the cremation of an object ensures supernatural life.

Then, carried on stretchers, came the friends' offerings: lacquered suckling pigs, fruits, and other delicacies.

These were followed by a procession of banners on which were inscribed the profession of the defunct and his merits (it goes without saying that he had only merits). "Was president of such and such an association . . . contributed generously to such and such other association." In short, a historical apologia for the departed.

Then more musicians, these playing the cymbal and other odd instruments.

They were followed by the carts, the first of which bore the wreaths. It, in turn, was followed by another much larger and more richly decorated vehicle: the hearse itself, on the roof of which was a kind of glazed gallery representing, in bright colors, mythological scenes (for the Westerner, it strangely recalled the colored panels that magicians set up over their booths at fairs). The bier lay in the middle of the chariot. In front sat the driver, or rather the truck driver, for the vehicle was simply a truck that had been transformed, but artfully camouflaged with richly embroidered cloths covering the wheels and, instead of mudguards, two green dragons undulating from front to back. The other half of the chariot served as a platform for the bonzes.

Behind the funeral wagon—on foot—were the members of the family, all wearing their hoods. First came the eldest son, wearing a kind of rice-straw crown and holding in his right hand a white stick signifying that it was he who was now the head of the family cell, the continuator of the cult, the link between the living and the dead. With his body leaning forward, he stumbled along, giving the impression that he was going to fall flat on his face at any moment. His dejection was such that two assistants—I am tempted to say accomplices—had to support him under the arms, for his head was wobbling limply as if he were distraught with grief. It does not matter whether the grief is real or not. The point is to manifest it, heartbreakingly. The Chinese is an incomparable actor when it comes to performing this role.

Then came the long procession of relatives, walking two by two and casually toying with their fans. They conversed tranquilly; the important thing was to keep in line.

They were followed by a file of trucks, the round hoods of which were lined with long banners laid side by side. These banners, which are the gifts of friends and acquaintances, are made of white cloth bearing inscriptions, some embroidered and some made of colored paper that is cut out and pasted on the cloth (the preparation of these strips is a big job; there are special shops in town which do only that). These streamers contain testimonials of friends to the departed person's qualities: "No better man has ever lived" . . . "His soul is still with us."

Then came the delegations of the societies and associations to which the deceased had belonged, each preceded by its banner.

A long line of friends brought up the rear.

The burial ceremony itself was no less complex and corresponded to the concrete way in which the Chinese views the soul. According to him, each individual is inhabited by two distinct souls. There is the "animal" soul (called by some the "spermatic" soul), which continues to inhabit the body after death. If one does not take all the necessary precautions with it, it may animate the corpse and even attack the living at night in order to drag them off to the grave. Then there is the higher soul, the "spiritual" soul, which goes to hell and, after a longer or shorter time, returns and takes its place in the home on the shelf of the ancestors. It is supposed to revisit the home before that, the first time on the third day after the burial to "go looking for the light of its eyes," and again between the ninth and nineteenth day of the month of decease, this time accompanied by "starveling" souls, which try desperately to reincarnate themselves. The family then summons the bonzes, who serve them a meal to pacify them and who, when the meal is over, take their sabers, which are made of wood or paper, and swing them about the room to make the surfeited souls depart from the dwelling.

During each lunar period there are rites for the dead. On the fifteenth day of the seventh moon there takes place the festival of the "Wandering Souls," including those of drowned persons who lie unburied. Lotus-shaped lanterns are lit and placed on the surface of the water, where they are set adrift in order to light up the way for souls in quest of reincarnation. This spectacle is exquisitely poetic.

At this point the reader may very well wonder why the Chinese subjects himself to such strict rules of behavior, so rigorous a "formulary of life." The answer, I think, is to be found in his history. China has always been an agricultural and overpopulated nation. As an agricultural nation, it functions in accordance with Nature and is in intimate union with her. For the Chinese "the ancestral soil is, at one and the same time, his history, memory and recollection. He can no more deny it than he can deny himself." [3] "For Chinese philosophy, Heaven and Earth, the unfolding of the universe and the life of mankind, ethics and the normal course of nature, form a *closed and single* system." The Chinese are more penetrated with this notion than any other people. For them, all things are linked. As Kayserling has said, he "has never opposed man to nature. He sees him as part of the latter." However mysterious he may seem (though the mystery exists only for the Westerner), he is more down to earth than anyone else. He is not an isolated element

[3] Kayserling, *Travel Journal of a Philosopher.*

but part of a whole, an extension of the soil from which he derives his force and knowledge.

Another thing that explains the behavior of the Chinese is overpopulation. To quote Kayserling again: "It is not possible, in a life in which people are so squeezed together as are the Chinese, to prosper if one lacks breeding. In China, a boor is hardly less dangerous than a common-law offender among us." Living together so closely requires constant prudence on the part of the individual. Hence the necessity for rules of conduct, which become ethics.

This is perhaps the most remarkable fact of all, for etiquette in China has not become, as it has elsewhere, a system of grimaces executed willy-nilly. It has become wisdom, a wisdom requiring respect for that which *is*. "Though it would be unreasonable to demand that everyone be virtuous and good, one is justified in demanding that each individual recognize fully the right of every other person to exist. This is the deeper meaning of courtesy. . . . Politeness is not an external form but rather the most elementary expression of morality. This meaning has been admirably developed in the *Book of Rites*, which declares that man cannot be perfect inwardly unless his outer behavior is perfect. It is considered to be self-evident that form symbolizes substance, that the outer expresses the inner." [4] Politeness, in this sense, becomes a virtue whose influence flows back to the individual himself. It becomes a system of betterment not only for society but for each of its members. "Manners maketh man." Ethics is not a commandment from on

[4] Ibid.

high, a law external to the individual, but an inner rule. To do nothing that might disturb one's neighbor and thus disturb the harmony of the whole is an injunction that the Chinese seems to obey instinctively.

Therein lies an entire cosmogonical concept. And the Chinese does not reason about his concept. He *lives* it. He lives his philosophy. And his philosophy makes of him not only a lover of form—as symbolic of substance —and of good—because to him the beautiful and the good are inextricable from each other—but also, because he sees everything in concrete form, an eminently functional being.

This concrete way of envisaging the universe is best expressed in the Chinese language. It was therefore urgent that I set about learning the language, if I wished to make contact, however little, with the Chinese "way." But what was I to do? I could not tackle the job without a master. But such a master would have to speak a European language if we were to communicate. To find such a person in Cholon was no easy matter. In any large Chinese city you will find Chinese who speak English, but not in Cholon. Not only that, but during the more than eighty years they have been under French influence they seem to have resolutely refused to learn French.

Finally some friends found a tutor for me, a Mr. Li. "He is a man of letters," I was told, "exactly the kind of person for you. He happens to be free at the moment."

I replied that I was "indeed most fortunate," and I asked—through an intermediary—whether Mr. Li would be so good as to take the trouble to come to my hotel.

At the appointed time Mr. Li presented himself cere-

"*Mister Li wore glasses, as befitted a scholar. He had an extremely long neck, and an Adam's apple strangely resembling that of the lizards . . .*"

moniously at my door. As befitted a "scholar," he wore
glasses. He had an extremely long neck and an Adam's
apple strangely resembling that of the lizards that
shared my room, in that it could go up and down without any other part of his body moving.

I invited him in and requested him to be seated. First
I served him tea, in accordance with the ritual. Mr. Li
placed himself at the edge of the chair and remained
there smiling. He was wearing cream-colored trousers
and a shirt of the same color hanging out of the trousers.
The only flaw in his attire was a pair of sickly green
down-at-the-heels shoes. But it would have been unseemly to stare at them too insistently, for I could feel at
once that Mr. Li was one of those Orientals who, in
order to impress their coreligionists, pretend, with a
quite Asiatic artfulness, to a knowledge that they do not
always possess but who are as sensitive as they are vain,
in the Chinese manner, of course—that is, with an ex-
aggerated modesty which makes one feel all the more
that they are "exceptionally" competent.

Mr. Li had been described to me as having "a superior knowledge of your language." Therefore, I would at
least be able, thanks to him, to work my way into
Chinese. But first we had to enter into contact to see
whether we "suited" each other.

No sooner had we begun to converse than I realized
that Mr. Li scarcely knew French. My Chinese friends
had thus been in error. But how were we to break off
without either of us losing face?

In order to get around the difficulty, I took from my
pocket a sheet of paper on which I had jotted down
questions about everyday matters. I handed it to Mr. Li,

who took it with a polite grin. His eyes moved slowly along the lines, but I felt that had he read them backward the result would have been the same. Seeing that I was observing him, he then assumed the annoyed look of a man who hears a mosquito buzzing about him, while focusing his attention on the page. Then, satisfied with his pantomime, he handed the sheet back to me with a broad grin, but without a word.

I then got up to look for three sheets of paper which I had found in my room upon my arrival at the hotel. Each of the sheets contained, above a date of the Chinese calendar, characters, brushed in by hand, of whose meaning I had no idea but the mere form of which delighted me and aroused my curiosity. I handed them to Mr. Li, requesting that he translate them for me.

"Well," said he, after fidgeting in his chair, "it's . . . about the 'girls.' This one, [pointing to the first sheet] is called Sut-mei. *Sut* means ice. A very pure thing. *Mei* means pretty, charming. . . . And this one, [a brief pause] is called Siu Zim-hong. That means little-superb-red. . . . The third is On-mei, that is, quiet-pretty."

Then he stared and grinned at me as one does at a person who has been making an ass of himself.

It was my turn to be embarrassed. What I had innocently taken for poetical inscriptions proved to be nothing other than the individual reference slips of prostitutes containing a physical description of the girl and her qualities!

That was as far as my Chinese lesson went. Mr. Li now assumed an attitude of detachment tinged with condescension. It was obvious that he and I had not "clicked" (a sensation as definite as it is imponderable).

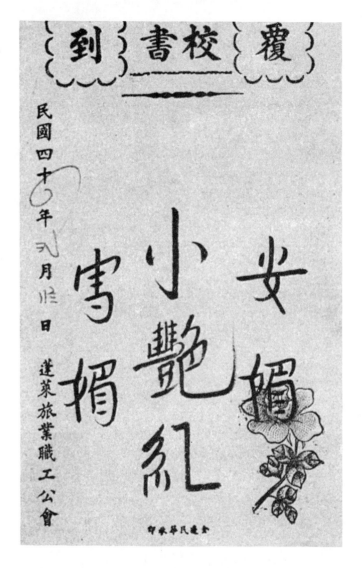

SUT-MEI   SIU-ZIM-HONG   ON-MEI

SUT: snow, purity   SIU: tiny   ON: quiet, comforting
MEI: lovely   ZIM: superb   MEI: lovely
                    HONG: red

"What I had innocently taken for poetical inscriptions—on the calendar sheets—were nothing other than the individual reference slips of prostitutes containing a physical description of the girl and her qualities . . ."

I let him go with a thousand thanks and the following morning informed the friends who had sent him that he was too scholarly for my inadequate knowledge and that to expect him to teach me even the rudiments of the Chinese language would be for him an ordeal that I really could not inflict upon him.

While waiting to find another teacher, I was obliged to manage as best I could alone.

I therefore remained in my room and plunged into my handbook. But though I wallowed about in it for hours on end, I felt myself getting bogged down. All my previous study of Lao-tse, and Mo-tse, and of the commentaries adapted to our Western understanding by Kou Hung-min, Lin Yutang, and others, were of no avail. Chinese is not a language as we understand the term. Its characters are not letters but signs. Each of them is the graphic, if not symbolic, representation of an idea and even a group of ideas. It involves a concept totally different from ours. And how difficult it is for a man to modify his concept. Our Western intelligence renders everything abstract, whereas the Chinese expresses everything, even the most abstract ideas, in concrete fashion. The following are examples drawn from my book:

土 The Prince — Three horizontal strokes representing heaven, earth and, between them, mankind. As the king's task is to establish the relationship among the three realms of the universe, he is represented by a vertical stroke uniting the three others.

142

旦 The Dawn   Above, heaven. Below, the horizon, symbolized by a stroke. Heaven is above the horizon.

雨 The Rain   Above, heaven, indicated by a horizontal stroke. Center, a cloud, represented by a curved stroke and four points, symbol of water. Connecting the two, a vertical stroke representing the fall of water.

Thus the idea "goodness" is represented by a woman and child; "peace," by a woman under a roof; "quarrel," by two women face to face.

As an example of how our thinking is expressed in Chinese, I shall list a few sentences with the approximate translation given in the handbook:

What time is it?	This moment is how many strokes of the clock?
I do not know him.	I, with him, not mutually knowing.
He thinks as you do.	He, in like manner, with you, is thus thinking.
How much does this desk cost?	This write-characters-table is what price money?
Do your best.	Employ yourself heart doing, very good, perfect.
Where should I put the butter?	This cow-oil, I should put in what place?

How are you?	Your body-body quiet-peace, eh?
He has a bad cold.	He cold his person, very serious.
Could you get me one like it?	You for me seek be able a similar one this one, same kind, or no?

I was appalled by the enormity of the task that lay before me. Hitherto I had flattered myself that I had a "gift for languages" and had even claimed that the more of them I learned the suppler grew my mind. But intellect has nothing to do with learning Chinese. It is not a matter of intellectual assimilation but of organic absorption. This visual universe had first to be incorporated into me, not by the brain but by the senses. I had to achieve the vision of the child who simultaneously absorbs and is absorbed by the object before him, and that of the poet who makes everything visible, "the web of the night" or the "mood of the stream." My impotence was all the more vexing in that the characters held an irresistible attraction for me. Even before I understood them they beckoned to me. Their very form invited me, though without my quite being able to localize the source of the invitation. It was like the call of waters—and indeed they have the fluidity and elusiveness of water. No sooner would I open my book than I would feel myself drawn in. It was like a forest, so dense that at its very edge I already felt myself lost, and also like an immense swamp that would suck me down. Each time I approached I felt a mingling of attraction and anxiety. At the end of an hour's study everything would be dancing before my eyes. I would be utterly exhausted. It was obvious that I would never manage alone.

Finally another teacher was proposed. I was told that he spoke English fluently. But he was extremely busy, what with business relationships between Chinese and Westerners, and his European pupils. "He may take you on anyway," I was told, "if he likes your looks."

This prelude worried me. Now, my face is as un-Asiatic as can be, owing to the fact that it reflects my most fleeting feelings. Furthermore, it is assymetrical—which is quite serious in the eyes of the Chinese, for whom harmony of features is all-important.

I was introduced to the new teacher by a European intermediary who brought us together in a neutral place to see whether I suited him. I must admit that even before meeting him I felt humiliated. Instead of being the "internationally known writer," I was merely a man who was humbly requesting, for a consideration, the favor of a few hours of tutoring.

But the man who was introduced to me was all smiles and very much at ease. His Chinese urbanity had obviously been heightened by contact with Europeans. He declared that he was delighted to meet me, with a smile that displayed his whole range of teeth. And although he was unable to take me on immediately, in view of his present engagements, he could not refuse, in view of the quality of the intermediary who had brought us together, to render me this service when he had time. I thanked him with repeated bows, for I was now beginning to get the hang of this gesture. On the other hand, what I did not yet know was how to ask him what his fee was. I finally risked it, very awkwardly. He smiled.

"Yes, yes!" he exclaimed. Then, after fidgeting for a moment, he added, "For one hour I usually take a thousand francs. For you, it will be two thousand."

I had difficulty repressing a start. Yet, as I knew, that was a simple matter of consideration for me. "I have no doubt of the fact," said the European friend who had brought us together, "that when you get under way the price will drop by at least half. Don't forget that in your relations with any Chinese there is the 'threshold' that must first be crossed."

XI

As FOR the importance that the Chinese attach to human relations, I was able to see for myself at my hotel.

At the beginning I had to pay daily—and in advance. The first thing the boyess did when she came to my room in the morning was to put out her hand and say, "Hundred forty piastres!" Not overbearingly, but as if it were simply a routine matter.

But after a while I had a devil of a time getting my bill. If I asked for it the immediate reaction was: "Ah, so you're leaving us?"

"No," I would assure them, "I'd merely like to pay what I owe."

My floor clerk, a good-humored chap who, thank heavens, spoke a bit of French, would raise his arms in protest.

"There's plenty of time!"—as if there were no rush at all and as if it would have been the height of indiscretion to manifest the slightest doubt as to my solvency.

"No mistake about it," I said to myself, "things have changed." Probably they had carried out a kind of investigation through channels unknown to me. There was, of course, the possibility that they had gone through my baggage to be sure I had money, and as I never locked anything it would have been easy to look through my things.

Nevertheless, when I did receive my bill, I felt suspicious. Perhaps they had dragged the affair out so as to make it impossible for me to verify the account. (It would have been typically Chinese to pluck me, if only to see what I was going to do about it!) But everything was in order. I was astounded. Could it mean, by any chance, that I was "in"? If so, what could have brought about the change? My curiosity was aroused, all the more so as there was no way of knowing. The Chinese, as I have said, is the most distrustful of men. Or rather, he believes everything and nothing. At first they must have taken me for the kind of Frenchman who is on the lookout for a "Chinese miss" and for whom a hotel of that kind is an ideal refuge. For just as they make it their business to know everything about you inside the hotel, in like manner they are perfectly discreet as far as the outside world is concerned, and if someone they don't know comes asking for you, they reply with an expression of utmost candor that they have never in their life seen you.

As I was alone, they assumed I needed someone. The contrary would have been unthinkable. If I refused the offer of such company that the boyess had made to me upon my arrival at the hotel, the reason probably was that I was tired. And so they waited until the following day to repeat the proposal, or rather, to remind me of the customs, for the Chinese is very eager to see you "enter" into his way of life.

Again I said no, smilingly. Whereupon they began studying me more attentively. Would I fancy a young boy? They were ready to go get me one then and there. (To them, the thing was as natural as wanting a woman.)

Not that either? The Chinese curiosity had been aroused. No woman . . . and pecking away at his type-writer all day long! They had come to examine it inside out. I can still see the boyess, unable to resist any longer, reaching out her hand to strike a key and, at the appearance of a letter on the blank sheet, being completely awe-struck. To the Chinese, the act of writing is such a live form of expression, such a direct emanation of a human being, that to see a machine produce writing was probably, in her eyes, a sort of magic.

Thus they had to know everything about how I lived. Privacy was impossible. They would not even wait for me to leave before coming to see. They'd push one of the swinging doors and in they'd troop. As for the youngsters, it was easier still. They had only to get down on all fours to observe from under the panels, for hours on end, the doings of the *sai yan*. And as for the boyess, the slightest pretext was sufficient for her to barge in.

"Did you ring? No? But surely you'd like some tea." And before I knew it she was pouring. "*Tcham tcha!*" Then: "What's that? You didn't have it yesterday!"

"A camera."

Her eyes lit up. "*Fô-to!*" (It becomes Chinese.) "Are you going to operate it?"

"No."

"Then you probably want a girl?" (They had not given up hope.)

I went back to my typing. She moved off, shaking her head. It was clear that I was a "scholar" (hence their consideration). But to sit there writing all day long! It wasn't normal! There was a time for everything, a time for idling, for taking a nap, for fornication (the Chinese calendar indicates them).

It all seemed so odd to them—that man who settled down in the midst of prostitution and mahjong to work—and so seriously! They simply couldn't stand it any longer. One afternoon the clerk appeared at my door with another Chinese.

"This is the Honorable Proprietor," he explained with a broad grin.

"That's odd," I said to myself. "I've never seen him! No doubt he's busy with other affairs." Every Chinese, from what I could see, had fingers in several pies. The publisher of the local paper was director of some rice warehouses in addition to being part owner of a hardware shop . . . and of a funeral parlor. As for the principal of the Canton School, he was also a partner in a laundry. Every individual was a spider with multiple arms.

"The Proprietor," continued the abacus man, "is most eager to make your acquaintance."

What else was there for me to do than to declare that I was deeply honored? I invited them to be seated and called for tea. And there they sat, smiling. What did they want?

Time went by. They kept smiling. Finally the abacus man spoke up. "The Proprietor," he said with a gesture of respect to his superior, "would like to know whether you feel at home here."

"Here it comes," I said to myself, "they're going to kick me out because I don't spend anything on extras." I didn't lose money at mahjong, I didn't send for girls. There was no denying the fact that I was a poor sort of guest.

Nevertheless I tried to appear self-possessed. "It couldn't be better," I replied.

They bowed in unison. "Very good, very good! And . . . you work a great deal, don't you?"

Was it simple curiosity on their part, or an investigation? Could the supposed Proprietor be, by any chance, a member of the police? "Calm down," I said to myself, "keep smiling."

"I've come here to study Chinese life, which attracts me most particularly."

"Ho-ho!" (in approbation). "And," said the abacus man, who was beside himself with curiosity, "it seems that you also draw."

"Yes, would you like to see my drawings?"

Before I finished my sentence they were on their feet. Their curiosity was at the breaking point. I ought to have known that anything involving the use of pen and ink thrills the Chinese.

But as soon as they looked at my sketches I could see they were disappointed. My way of seeing was not theirs. They did not understand it. A moment later they were on their way out, excusing themselves politely. But if there was anything I needed . . .

However, for all that, the observation of me continued. Whenever I left my room to go to town I could feel that everything was noted, the look on my face, what I wore (my rope-soled Basque sandals quite intrigued them), particularly as, in going from my room to the street, I had to pass a good fifty persons.

When I got to the street I would frequently meet one of my floor boys. There were two of them. This one was the specialist in discreet errands. He was always ready for anything, provided you made your request with a dash of humor. The other one was a lean youngster with very clear skin. Whenever he served my tea he would brush against me. And each time he would linger for a moment. . . . I acted as if I didn't understand. God, how confusing those *sai yan* were! I could detect the reproach in both their faces. "Don't you ever take anyone?"

They would gladly have pardoned my being a bad guest, from a monetary point of view. What they could not quite pardon was my behavior. It was unethical. Every art has its rules. Here the rules required that you do "like everyone else." But I did nothing like everyone else. Despite the fact that I was cultivated—and the Chinese notices this at once, even if your culture is not his—and that I had a friendly word to say when I walked through the lobby, I did not "function," and to "function" is Rule Number 1 of Chinese life. To function means to behave like a healthy, normal individual. The more you function the better you feel. To function—according to your personal nature—is not fatiguing but restful. Nothing is better than to spend oneself . . . and to spend money so as to make the world go round. It's a sign of naturalness. And of sociability. To the Chinese, remaining alone is a sign of sickness. God knows what that can lead to! Probably to repression. In any case, to humorlessness.

Now humor is of prime importance in life. That's why the Chinese fear passion in love. It isolates human beings; it is therefore anti-social. If a man is caught up in passion, his friends quickly try to find him some ravishing creature in order to divert him and bring him back to the circuit.

I was aware of all this, particularly as my European friends kept commenting on my behavior.

"Are you still alone at your hotel?" one would ask very casually. "Aren't you . . . tempted," another would query, "to try a bit of a sample?" And a third would hint, "Are you quite satisfied? Isn't there anything you need?" The acclimatized European always derives a certain malicious satisfaction from watching the greenhorn adapt himself.

Finally I came out with what was in the back of my mind. "What I'd like is not Chinese women but *a* Chinese woman. The prostitutes may be very charming, but they won't give me what I'm looking for. The taxi girls? Yes, I admit that there are some very pretty ones, but it takes a great deal of patience, according to you, before you can take them out. I'd rather save my patience for a woman of good family, if ever I have the luck to find one."

They shook their heads. "If that's what you're after, my boy, that's a horse of another color. Your idea is, in itself, a very good one, but not, I'm afraid, very practical."

As I started to protest, exclaiming that after all I was a gentleman and my intentions were perfectly honest, and as I even went so far as to say, in my irritation, that "it could hardly be considered a dishonor to be seen with me," they tried to set me straight.

"To find what you're looking for, you'd have to get into the 'right sort' of circle in Cholon, but such circles are completely closed. They don't give a rap about even the 'right sort' of foreigner. In fact they're wary of Europeans. More than one Chinese in Cholon bitterly regrets ever having received them, because they were indiscreet or tired to sleep with the daughter of the family. Being invited to a restaurant is easy. But it takes a trick or two to get into a Chinese home. You'll never be able to manage it except through a European who can introduce you. But very few Europeans here enjoy the confidence of the Chinese. And those who do would be reluctant to introduce you, especially into the home of people whose friends they have become. Such friendships are won with great difficulty, and they're very jealous of them. And, besides, they'd be afraid that if ever you misbehaved they would lose face among friends whom they care more about.

"But first you need a name! The very first thing to do when you meet a Chinese is to give him your card, with your European name on one side and your Chinese name on the other. So long as you don't have a Chinese name you won't have any identity for them."

Indeed, that was true. I did not yet have a name! Kindly friends had, however, tried to find one for me. But you must not imagine that finding a name is a simple matter. It had already been the subject of two whole sessions at a table in a restaurant, at the rear, in order to be away from the noise.

Before putting anything on paper my friends began by plunging themselves into a state of meditation, in the Chinese manner. First they had to steep themselves in the problem; then to breathe slowly and regularly, so as to clear the way to that tranquil lake of the spirit where images well up effortlessly. From time to time one of them would look up and contemplate me thoughtfully, and then would resume his meditation. Suddenly, as if a window had just opened within him, he would rapidly draw some strokes . . . De Poncins . . . Tai Pong-san.

Here I must pause for an explanation, for the finding of the Chinese name is an infinitely subtle affair. It is a matter not simply of transcribing the European sound phonetically, in three characters—no more, no less—but also of rendering the person's quality, not his physical quality, as was done among us in the old days by tacking on a descriptive nickname, such as George the Dwarf or Charles the Bald, but the intrinsic quality of the man. A prostitute, for example, might be called "Fragile Little Dearness of the Heart" or "Discreet Perfumed Temple." The outer appearance is combined with the very essence of the person, in other words, the deeper harmony between the visible and non-visible.

My friends looked at each other inquiringly. They were holding an unspoken consultation in my presence. . . . Tai Pong-san? No, it wouldn't do! Though the sounds rendered my name phonetically, they did not correspond to what I was. But, all things considered, what was my veritable self?

They reverted to my face. They tried to see me as some transparent substance in order to perceive my deeper self, or rather my most essential self. So there I sat, feeling more and more uneasy, at the back of the restaurant, the object of their leisurely scrutiny. It reminded me of the observation to which I had once been subjected by a psychiatrist. He had looked me up and down in an attempt to get some notion of my heredity and physical defects, lingered for a moment on my hands, shifted his gaze to my face, studying all its aspects, as if it were a relief map, in an effort to get an over-all picture. But my friends were going much further than that, were probing more deeply. What they were trying to do was to determine the spirit that governed my being and to see the color of my personality. What signs would represent it? The sign "Receptivity-Sensitivity-Vital Drive"? Or, since the element earth was dominant in me, the sign "Earth-Root-Obstinacy"?

Having rejected Tai Pong-san, they looked elsewhere. "By what name do people usually call you?"

"Mike," I replied.

They were off again with Mai-ke. But the third term was not forthcoming.

Finally one of the experts stood up. "I've got to be going. I'll think about your case."

And there the matter rested. I was a person without identity. And as long as I had none I would not exist! That was what suddenly struck me in the presence of the person who had come to discuss the problem with me.

"Besides," he continued, with ever so faint a touch of sarcasm, "there's no absolute certainty that they'll like you. The Chinese, as you know, goes less by the beauty or ugliness of a person's features than by the general harmony. That's something that we Westerners are not sufficiently sensitive to. For example, if some of our Western women don't like the long nose they've been blessed with, they have it shortened. Suddenly they realize everything's wrong! Simply because the new nose, however pretty it may be, no longer 'goes' with the rest. They're worse than Cyrano! Because Cyrano's nose, enormous though it was, expressed the man and was wonderfully in harmony with the rest of his face. And harmonious ugliness is far preferable to dissonant beauty. What appeals chiefly to the Chinese is unity. If anything about your features disturbs him, he will be on the defensive.

"Another thing. Your behavior. You can be very charming one day and sullen the next. And what's even worse is that you make no effort to conceal your shifts of mood. Being even-tempered is quite indispensable here. If ever the Chinese senses the least bit of impatience or nervousness, you're through.

"And even if you manage to correct these short-comings, you can't be sure of getting what you're after. Even the taxi girls hesitate to go out with a white man. The fact of being seen with him makes her lose caste in the eyes of her companions. With a girl of 'good family' the difficulty is even greater. Going out with you, even if she should want to, would be a challenge, and she would have to justify her doing so by the excellence of your behavior. You'd be constantly on pins and needles, particularly as your inadequate knowledge of Chinese life might cause you to make all sorts of blunders. And, believe me, they would be promptly noted. The girl wouldn't say anything to you, of course. She'd be much too fine for that, but nevertheless you would alienate her."

Nevertheless I let it be known at my hotel that I was in quest of a girl of good family. There was no reaction, save for the peculiar Chinese laugh, which you do not know how to interpret. Was my project absurd? Of course, and they were unable to understand why I didn't take life simply when all about me was everything I needed. Could one possibly imagine a man who had the means to live a full and hearty life and did not take advantage of his good fortune?

However, wind of the matter must have got around town, for on a number of occasions Chinese acquaintances would say to me, "So you're looking for a wife," and would then change the subject.

And there the matter rested when, one day, receiving a visit at my hotel from a friend who was married to a Chinese woman, I said "Let's send for the manager. We'll invite him to have a drink with us and then we'll lay the matter before him . . . just to see what happens."

The manager arrived, smiling as usual, though wondering what it was we wanted of him. When the preliminaries were over my friend said to him in a bantering tone, "Well? Aren't you going to find a well-bred girl for my friend here?"

The man fidgeted a bit. "Of course," he answered, "but it's quite difficult." He seemed anxious to get away as fast as he could.

"You're putting these people into an impossible situation," my friend explained to me. "You don't even touch the women they have here for your pleasure, and you ask them to find you a 'decent' girl. In the first place, that's not at all their line. And besides, what would be in it for them? They'd have nothing to gain and everything to lose. They're tradesmen, and you musn't forget it!"

And that was that. However, in my relations with the

hotel I did try to redeem my peculiarity by handing out substantial tips. I might add that the better they came to know me the more considerate they were. To be sure, they regarded me as an odd fish, but so long as I did not interfere with the social order, that was my own affair.

XII

However different Cholon and Saigon are from each other, they are nevertheless commercially interdependent. From Cholon comes rice, from Saigon manufactured products. The Chinese businessman who has his warehouses in Cholon is to be found in Saigon every morning, at the stroke of eleven, on the sidewalk near the Bank of Indo-China, for the Rice Exchange. Thus there is a constant flow back and forth between the two cities, and this explains the importance of the means of transport.

There are three types of vehicle: the taxis, the rickshaws driven by motorized bicycle, and those driven by ordinary bicycle.

I shall not speak of the taxi drivers. As they possess "an auto," they are as disdainful as the others are humble. They are no longer hungry, whereas the others are still marked by the pathos of the starveling.

Some of the rickshaw boys are Vietnamese, others Chinese. But they are rickshaw boys first and foremost.

If there can be said to be a caste apart here, it is theirs; in fact one wonders whether they ever mingle with the others. They have *their* street corners where they wait in line, though with no personal contact among themselves, as if they were all isolated beings. They have their alleys, where they sleep, slumped in their vehicles, and their stalls, where they go for a bite, sitting on the curb beside the stall with a bowl of rice in their palms.

Among them can be seen all sorts of physical types. There is the kind who, with sober dignity, wears the helmet—very soiled—of the white man, and who sits bolt upright as he pedals, like a circus monkey riding round a ring.

There is the one who wears big blue glasses, the intellectual, the man of the colonial intelligentsia, superior to the others because of his primary-school certificate. His hollow chest is consumed with tuberculosis and hatred. He is the man who one of these days will "fling the colonialists into the sea," but until then he will remain perfectly quiet, for prudence is imperative. His lips are thin, his nostrils pinched—signs of the revolutionary violence that is brewing, the outer symbol of which is the hat of the Vietnamian guerrillas, with the brim turned up at a defiant angle. He has a motor-driven vehicle that spits and sputters, leaving behind a sickening train of smoke. He drives it with his chest drawn in, objectively, if I may say so, in contrast with the simple rickshaw boys who toil away subjectively. He will not even deign to look at you and pockets the fare coldly, as if waiting grimly for the Great Day to arrive.

A third type is the good-natured fellow, the decent sort of native, totally devoid of meanness—and of thought

"There is the kind who, with sober dignity, wears the helmet—very soiled—of the white man, and who sits bolt upright as he pedals, like a circus-monkey riding round a ring . . ."

"There is the one who wears big blue glasses, the man of the colonial intelligentsia . . ."

"A third type is the good-natured fellow, totally devoid of meanness— and of thought as well. He drives you along with his honest calves, and smiles as you dismount, whatever the tip you give him . . ."

as well. He drives you along with his honest calves and smiles as you dismount, whatever the tip you give him. As soon as he has a few pennies he treats himself to some lemonade, which he drinks like a horse.

As for the "colonial" type, here are some notes on a few specimens, all of indefinable race:

The sub-man. His expression is a complete blank. Wears a peaked American cap that heightens his blankness. Pushes with all his being, looking neither to right nor left. Lives on bamboo shoots, parts of which he spits out in long jets of brownish saliva.

The long stringbean. Lean and rawboned. So dry that he never perspires. His thighs are like sticks of wood. Yet he is nonetheless colorful, with his khaki shirt, English army shorts, and Australian hat cocked forward. He is of the type dear to Kipling, loyal and devoted to his chief, as were the natives of the heroic age. He is utterly tireless, animated not by his legs but by his devotion, and awaits only a sign from you to start pedaling, roaring all other vehicles out of the way to bring you gloriously to your destination.

Then there is the "exotic type," with chocolate complexion and woolly hair, wearing the Tonkinese hat that looks like a parasol. On his back, a loose-fitting, cool-looking shirt. On his feet, sandals, held in place by the big toe. A corncob pipe between his teeth. He is the man whom the tourist chooses infallibly. His outfit is a sure-fire come-on. Drives his customers through the picturesque quarters, the Big Market, the Botanical Garden, as if the whole town were laid out to meet his needs. A congenial fellow, ready to talk, who pockets his tip with a grin.

Lastly there is the Asiate, strange and mysterious. He

"As for the 'colonial' type, there is the long string bean. Lean and raw-boned. His thighs are like sticks of wood. Yet he is none the less colorful with his khaki shirt, English army shorts and Australian hat cocked forward . . . The type dear to R. Kipling: utterly tireless, animated not by his legs but his devotion . . ."

"The sub-man. His expression is a complete blank. Wears a peaked American cap that heightens his blankness . . . Lives on bamboo shoots, parts of which he spits out in long jets of brownish saliva . . ."

"There is also the 'exotic' type with chocolate complexion and wooly hair, wearing the Tonkinese hat that looks like a parasol . . ."

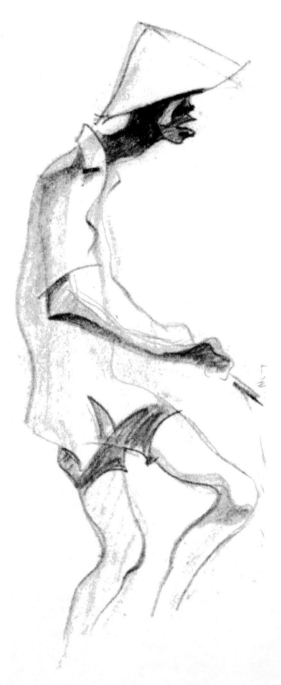

"*Lastly there is the Asiate, strange and mysterious. He does not evoke laughter, and there is no telling what goes on in his head . . .*"

does not evoke laughter. Rather, he tends to make you feel uneasy. There is no way of telling what goes on in his head. (Some tourists, however, like that sort of thing; it gives them a thrill.) Has a long hairless body. Gleaming cheekbones under his slits of eyes. His face, half hidden beneath his broad-brimmed rice-straw hat, is full of glints. His body is as supple as rubber. As he pedals along with his knees out, he looks, from behind, like a swimming frog.

But what is interesting is not so much the physical type as the behavior of the species and the psychology underlying its movements. However useful the rickshaw boys may be to society—without them communication between the two towns would be completely cut off—they are nevertheless all pariahs of a sort, treated like an inferior breed and tolerated with ill-concealed impatience. No sooner does a group of them collect at a street corner or opposite a big hotel than a policeman chases them away—with his club, if they do not obey promptly enough. They move off like birds of ill omen, only to gather elsewhere and again be driven away. But their capacity for putting up with things is infinite, as is their patience. Theirs is the hungry waiting at corners, with the watchful immobility of the Oriental, who observes the slightest movements, alert to the slightest expression of a desire. But as they are forbidden, under penalty of losing their license, to push themselves forward, they offer their services dumbly. The rickshaw boys have developed an art of soliciting, almost of prayer. One will point slyly to his cab, which he has polished temptingly. Another lets you know, with a simple gesture, that he is hungry. A third straightens up his body as if to say, "At your orders,

"It is particularly when darkness sets in that rickshaw boys loom large on the scene."

sahib!" The lucky one rushes forward while the others look on with oriental fatalism.

However, it is particularly when darkness sets in that the rickshaw boys loom large on the scene. When Saigon begins to fall into a state of bourgeois drowsiness, Cholon stirs with night life. The animation of the day is followed without transition by the swarming of the night. The Jade Palace is already packed with feverish diners, and the boys are careful to keep the fever at a high pitch. Outside, human beings flow by, animated by the vital drive so peculiar to China. Soon the dance halls will be opening. The taxi girls are already making their way along the main stem of town, one by one, each in her rickshaw, hieratic figures, not hostesses going off to their jobs, but idols being taken swiftly and fugitively to the temple.

It is the magic hour when the inscriptions in Chinese characters stand out in the darkness like gleaming rubies, when people, including those who relish good food, sit down at the street stalls in front of wondrous dishes: lacquered ducks that gleam like mummies lighted from within; fish bladders, light as sponges; twisted pig entrails. The nimble-fingered vendors, their bodies shining with sweat, are feverishly busy. Each shop casts its own bright light; each offers its particular temptation to lure the passer-by. It is the hour when Cholon is at its height. So potent is the "anima" issuing from the city that it is almost stifling. Its pulsation is not the powerful, noisy throbbing of our big cities, but something violent, almost virulent, that arises from each individual and clutches at your vitals. But there is nothing morbid about it. Everywhere else pleasure seems to have a flavor of sin, a suggestion of vice. Here everything is free. Human desires are liberated from the shackles and scruples of conscience. They are all licit, by virtue of the fact that they exist.

The rickshaw boys stand by, ready to serve you. You had simply been drifting along, immersed in the tide, indecisive but full of vague desires. The rickshaw boys are ready to give them form. "The girls are pretty at such and such a night club. . . . And the Chinese madam at such and such a house . . ." They know lots of places, at least so they tell you.

Are you slow in answering? They go even further. "French lady, husband on leave!" Or, "Beautiful lady, husband killed at Dienbienphu!" As the night advances they look more and more haggard, shadows springing to your side from the darkness.

The streets empty, the lights go out, the magic disappears and leaves behind the thick darkness. Cholon finally goes to sleep, amidst whiffs of grease and scents of spices, mingled with the pungent odor of opium. The rickshaw boys are still wandering about, their hunger never appeased. They are the wanderers of the night, the phantoms of the darkness.

At times I would return home very late. The streets would be empty, absolutely deserted. Suddenly I would hear a "Pst!" behind my back. A phantom, sprung from the shadow, pedaling noiselessly. The phantom rides beside me. Then: "Saigon, twelve piastres!" Since I am a white man, that's where I must be going.

No answer. The voice drops a tone, becomes more stealthy. "Saigon, ten piastres!"

I scowl. The phantom slinks back into the shadow, puts a prudent distance between itself and me, though

"Begging is a social fact, which has to be recognized . . . Further-more, the beggar is neither intrusive nor otherwise troublesome, even if he stands near your table for a good half hour . . ."

without abandoning me. Now it is reproach that follows me, until I am smitten by remorse.

There is another category of individuals whose time is devoted to the honorable trade of begging. On Jaccareo Street alone there are a dozen of them plying their craft in all tranquillity, for here there is nothing dishonorable in begging. It is a social fact, and the Chinese not only recognizes it but feels a moral obligation to give to the poor, if only to gain the good will of the spirits. And even if he does not give—for the same beggar approaches you ten times in the course of an evening —he is nevertheless extremely tolerant of the man who stands before him. Furthermore, the beggar is neither intrusive nor otherwise troublesome, even if he stands near your table for a good half hour. Most of the time he is waiting not for money but for the scraps of your meal. You will not find here those professional whiners who disguise themselves as scarecrows to force your generosity. Begging here is more discreet. Take that blind person, still a young man, moving along rapidly, guided by a child. When he reaches a table where people are dining his guide leaves him, very discreetly, and calls for him later. And the blind man does not stand before you as a reproach but merely as a social fact that ought to be considered.

Take that other, who moves as in a dream. He is an opium addict and obviously in the last stages of addiction. His Adam's apple is suspended in the form of a pocket and there is a hole under his cerebellum. As for his chest, he can hardly be said to have one; he has only a sinuous spinal column. And the sweater he is wearing

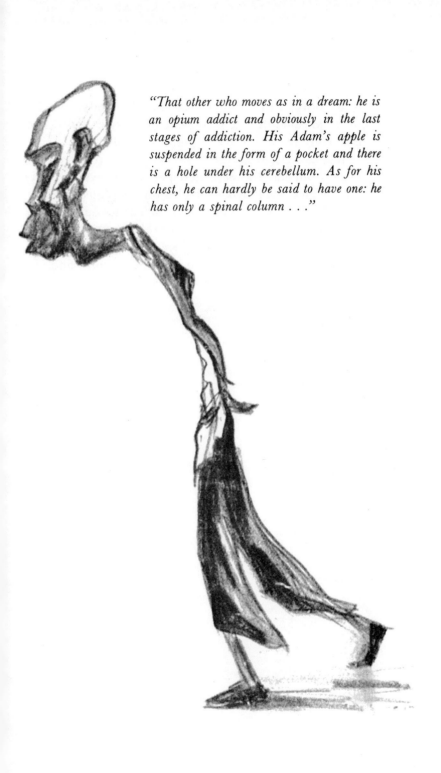

"That other who moves as in a dream: he is an opium addict and obviously in the last stages of addiction. His Adam's apple is suspended in the form of a pocket and there is a hole under his cerebellum. As for his chest, he can hardly be said to have one: he has only a spinal column . . ."

is not only in rags but is rotting on his body. One has the impression that he is propelled by spokes, for he cannot really be said to have thighs and calves.

Just as I rise from the table he looms up like a thief, takes from his pocket a newspaper (always the same one), whisks away what remains on the plate, and scurries off. It is not for himself that he carries out his raids, for he no longer eats, but to sell his booty to a starveling so that he himself can buy drugs. His utterly vacant air is that of a man who is no longer of this world and who returns to it only "for memory's sake."

XIII

WHATEVER his physical debility, the Chinese retains a surprising inner vitality. The most astonishing expression of this deep-seated drive that I ever witnessed was that of a cripple. And what a cripple! One of his legs, completely shriveled and atrophied from the trunk down, was folded under his buttocks. The other limb was even worse, for there was no flesh on either the thigh or leg, only shriveled skin that clung to the bone. The knee, of course, was wider than the rest and looked like a ball. With his hand on his knee, he would swing his leg around as if it were a pummeled cane. Buttressing his body on the other hand, which leaned on the ground and acted as a pivot, he would lift himself up and bound forward. In three hops he would cross the street—and faster than anyone else. When he reached the open door of the restaurant where I was seated he would cross the threshhold with an effortless lift.

Though half the man's body was dead, his gaze was

strangely alive, and even joyous. In view of the fact that he was so good-humored—and, as it were, well balanced —he was a great favorite, and people immediately would ask him to shine their shoes, for he was a bootblack and carried his equipment in a box slung across his back. He would set to work in a flash, occasionally looking up with a bright gaze. At first I had felt shy about staring at his limbs. But he was so "healthy" that in no time— unable as I was to converse with him—I felt not the slightest embarrassment in observing the high spirits with which he, a man who normally should have been a ruin, lived his life. As soon as he pocketed my three piastres he would take leave of me with a smile and slide over to the next table where another client was waiting.

But where do the Chinese get their vitality? What is the source of that resistance displayed even by those who look as if they could hardly stand on their feet?

I recall a man I used to see regularly on Jaccareo Street, a very textbook image of rickets. And yet he was a street porter. A good part of his day was spent delivering logs, one in front and one in back—balanced on U-curved bamboo slats—and the balancing pole in the middle. Each time he bent to pick up his load, I thought he would never get up, but the fact that he had a permanent stoop merely facilitated the carrying. When he had transported his wood, he would go about offering to do other jobs: unloading fish or cases of beer at the central market. I never saw him pause for breath or wipe his brow and look about for sympathy. Where was his motor? I often wondered.

I recall another, a cobbler, who was not only rachitic

but, judging from his stumpy gums, must also have had scurvy. Sitting on the sidewalk with his back to the wall and a pile of shoes all about him, he would sew and hammer and scrape from dawn to dark. I once took a photograph of him and gave him a copy, and thereafter we were friends, despite our being unable to converse. Whenever I went by he smiled at me. Although his smile was little more than a painful contraction, nevertheless it lit up his entire being. It was an expression of sound mental health. Whatever their debility, these people are essentially healthy. And they are virile, unlike so many other Orientals who are ambiguous.

In any case one thing is certain: the Chinese is well balanced. Not only is he neither frustrated nor anxious, but whatever he does, he does wholeheartedly, with a fullness of life that it is difficult for Westerners even to imagine. Look at his laughter. It is a veritable gush, an explosion of his entire person. And the way he eats. He does not pick at his food; he tackles it. His whole self is involved. The same intensity is manifested when he plays mahjong. Not only his brain but the whole man is engaged in the game. How else can one explain his capacity for grasping the position of 144 tiles, arranging several combinations at the same time and riposting like lightning? All kinds of things go into a game of mahjong. Mahjong satisfies not only the sense of finesse, which the Chinese applies to human relations as well as to business dealings, but also his passion for playing against chance. It is a means of practicing his philosophy, a training in equanimity, for though the game enthralls him, he must be able to lose with a smile and thereby dominate fate.

Another thing that seems to me to contribute to the

health of the Chinese is his ability to relax. I recall that
when I went back to the Sun Wah after lunch I would
find the managers wallowing in the lobby, in postures that
expressed not only nonchalance but a flaunting of their
entire being. One would be stretched his whole length,
with his toes spread fanwise; the other, a short, tubby
fellow, would tuck one leg under his belly, while holding
the other in both hands. A third would scratch his toes
blissfully, while his neighbor energetically rubbed his
gums with a stick (the Chinese go in a good deal for all
kinds of massage). However lacking in decency their postures might have seemed—all the more so in that they
had rolled up their trouser legs so as to be cooler—none
of them ever dreamed of making a move when I approached. They rather grinned, as if inviting me to do
likewise—me, the Westerner, who seemed to them tense
and contracted.

This indolence, however, is that of animals, which,
though they may seem asleep, can be up and alert in a
split second. You may go into a Chinese shop and find
the proprietor dozing. There is nothing to indicate that
he is even aware you have entered. Yet if you make the
slightest remark he is at once wide awake and all ears.

However absorbed the Chinese may seem, his curiosity
is always alert. The slightest unaccustomed detail is
enough to attract his attention. I had only to reach into
my pocket for a pencil to have an audience. They *had* to
see. In the restaurant where I usually ate, the boss, a fat
fellow, would rest his paunch on my table to observe at
ease what I was doing. Whether I liked it or not, I was
obliged to sketch with a belly in front of me.

As for working in the street . . . One day, on leaving

"In the restaurant where I usually ate, the proprietor, a fat fellow, would rest his paunch on my table to observe at ease what I was doing. Whether I liked it or not, I was obliged to sketch with a belly in front of me . . ."

the hotel, I stopped to draw the bridge. In a moment the rubbernecks were all about me. As they impeded my freedom of movement (some were even leaning on my shoulder in order to see better), I took refuge against the low wall that ran along the hotel. But that didn't bother them. They scaled the wall . . . until part of it collapsed. I immediately went in to tell the manager, as I felt somewhat responsible for the damage. Do you think he got angry? Not at all. He found the incident very funny.

Regarding the capacity of the Chinese for concentration: "Go visit Mr. Tai Wan-kiun in Cholon," I was advised. Mr. Tai Wan-kiun (Mr. Very Stable Authority) was a young man whose eyes sparkled with shrewdness and who, from all appearances, was richly endowed with vital energy. He had studied painting in the north of China with the best teachers until he discovered the miniature ivory carvings of the Ming period. To be a miniaturist in ivory—a substance in itself very difficult to work with—is a *tour de force,* for the artist cannot even see what he sculpts on the ivory!

Mr. Tai Wan-kiun therefore worked only at night, when absolute silence made it possible for him to attain the maximum concentration. Like all Chinese artists, he first created an inner calm in order to allow his vision of the object to focus more sharply. (For the Chinese does not reproduce nature; he creates landscapes dictated by his inner vision.) Then he "released his inner drive" through his arm, for the hand, in his case, was merely the blind executant. Once he engraved a poem of three thousand words on a piece of ivory two and a half inches square. And, what is even more remarkable, he carved a thirteen-line poem on a grain of rice!

Some of Mr. Tai Wan-kiun's works took several weeks to finish. They might well have taken months. It is interesting, in this connection, to quote what Mr. Abel Bonnard has said about working with jade:

"In view of the duration of human life, the worker spends what seems to be a disproportionate amount of time. . . . But he attaches himself, with an insistent and, as it were, adherent curiosity, to the object he wishes to reproduce. We no longer know what occult prestige, what muted importance, can be communicated to a human work by the duration of the effort that produces it and by the self-effacement of the craftsman. The work of art ends by being the equal of that of nature, both having been accomplished in the same *revels of patience.*"

Speaking, however, of jade—the favorite stone of the Chinese because its texture is peculiarly suggestive of a woman's skin—I should like to quote Mr. Vuong Hong-sen, a great connoisseur of art and the curator of the Saigon Museum:

"Among the most beautiful jades, the Chinese distinguish:

jade of a green called 'kingfisher'
jade of a blue-green called 'willow leaf in springtime'
jade of a green called 'melon rind'
jade of a new green
jade of a light emerald green
jade of a shrimp green
jade of a string-bean green
jade of a green called 'washed sky after rain'

"The jades most sought after, however, are those bearing traces of corrosions produced by the earth. These are said to be 'impregnated with blood spots.'

"According to a belief dear to scholars more steeped in poetry than in science, jade is the offspring of an elect stone that gestates in the earth for ages. Its value depends on its purity, veins, and color. According to the same scholars, its birth, which is a mysterious phenomenon, arises out of the slow and continuous action upon the stone by underground energies. Then, after a longer or shorter period of time, the stone assumes vague human, animal, and vegetable forms. . . . Just as lead is transformed to gold, so stone is transformed to jade because both these substances have magical power. Thus, when the Vietnamese or Chinese cast in bronze or sculpt in precious stone or wood the image of a god or genie, they are careful to place a little gold or a precious stone—jade or diamond—in the statue's belly in order to make it 'celestial' (*t'ien*). These two substances are supposed to be the abode of potent magical forces. When shut into the statue, they communicate to it their supernatural properties, like a burning ember."

Thus Chinese sense perceptions appear infinitely subtle. Perhaps this is to be explained by their age-old cultivation of their faculties. In this they recall certain primitives who, like animals, can smell the odor of fear or sickness. Or specialists in any society who, by dint of intensive training, are sometimes capable of the most incredibly subtle perceptions. (I once knew, for example, a specialist in perfumes who, when he entered a restaurant, could smell the individual odor of each woman present and could tell whether her perfume was right for her skin.)

But the odd thing about the Chinese is that though his olfactory sense is so developed that he can detect changes of mood from a person's bodily exhalation, he is, on the other hand, utterly insensitive to certain odors; for example, the smell of urine or decay seems not to affect him at all.

Is his morphology different from ours, as is that of gypsies? How, in view of the fact that he is so underfed, are we to explain his exceptional resistance? Why is his pulse beat slower than ours and why is his perspiration different, as physiologists say it is?

What is the reason for his curious physical insensitivity, which so many observers have noted? Opium, undernourishment, and rickets apparently ought to reduce his genetic capacity. Yet the Chinese are the most prolific people on earth.

How does the food he eats influence his vitality? The least that can be said is that Chinese cookery is highly uncommon. The first time I ate alone in a Chinese restaurant on Jaccareo Street, I could not refrain from copying the menu:

> Fish tripe, sponge style, with sauce
> Swallow's-nest soup, crab eggs
> Bladder soup with chicken feet
> Peacock consommé
> Shark fins with flower of cinnamon
> Chicken soup, bamboo shoots
> Fresh-water turtle with almonds
> Shrimps with almond flowers
> Chicken wing with oyster sauce
> Chicken with red-pepper rind

Pigeon stuffed with swallow's nests
Duck tongue sauté
Duck with dragon herbs
Pigeon with asparagus and bamboo
Iced water-lily seeds
Chinese rose wine

If some smart-aleck, speaking of Chinese recipes, were to say: "Take the pupils of the eyes of young pink flamingoes, brown slowly in iguana broth and serve with a lotus-flower sauce," he would be adding nothing to reality, at least not in a country where "hundred-year eggs" are served as a delicacy (they are steeped in ammonia until the yellows turn black and gummy). What would he say on learning that those excellent little things he was crunching were fried cockroaches? I have made mention, in speaking of the physical appearance of certain Chinese, of turtles, lizards, and iguanas. It so happens that these are their favorite foods. On entering a restaurant, you will find cages containing turtles, iguanas, and mongooses, and even poisonous snakes, ready to be sacrificed upon request.

What "virtues" does each of them contain? I asked the question, very prudently, of Mr. Tcheng, whom I took to lunch one day, hoping that I could also get him to talk about not only the nutritive but also the therapeutic and even aphrodisiac qualities of the various foods. Mr. Tcheng informed me that the duck, for example, was highly appreciated by the Chinese because it was the bird that could move on land, on and under water, and in the air; in short, it was the "complete" bird. Apart from this, he remained evasive, and rightly so, for, to the Chinese, cookery is not an isolated domain but part of a concept too universal, too subtle, to be grasped by a Westerner. My companion could clearly not have gone into the subject without speaking also of the *Tao* and the correspondences. He would also have had to speak about "noble" foods, in the sense used by the occultists of old who thought that individuals who were noble ate only the more delicate and subtler parts of animals. "Only the king," says Granet, in his *Chinese Thought*, "has precious food, according to the Hong Fan. His doctors combine flavors for him. And the Prime Minister—who should be versed in the culinary art—feeds the 'royal virtue,' the *Wang Tao*, in the person of his sovereign. He organizes the tribute so that nothing is lacking to compose his master's soul, that is, to sustain an authority that will be as entire, as 'one,' as little perishable, as possible. In combining the meats of the five domestic animals, five vegetable foods, five odors, and five flavors, he will repair, in accordance with a rhythm that is in conformity with the Order of the World, the five viscera, the proper functioning of which will be verified by inspecting the nine openings and by examining, with the aid of the five sounds and five colors, the five exhalations."

This is a far cry from simple gastronomy. It is a therapy in every sense of the term. The same can be said for music. In the words of Li Ki, "It stirs the blood and its conduits, sets the vital spirits circulating." By means of music "a harmonious equilibrium is established between the blood and the breath." The same obtains in regard to physical love, for it enables man and woman to "mingle their sexual liquors."

When a man, in accordance with the Chinese code, has spent his vitality to another's advantage, he must regain it in one way or another. Cookery is one such way, par excellence. And the belief, prevalent among all peoples, that if one eats certain organs of a man possessing vitality, strength, courage, and the like he may acquire a portion of these qualities, has always existed in China. Bull's testicles are a sovereign cure for impotence. Squab gives vitality, for it is the bird that has more of this quality than any other. Pig or goat liver is healthful for the human liver. The bile of a bear strengthens the sight.

Chinese pharmacopoeia fills volumes, for the race has accumulated the most minute observations over the centuries. As long ago as 3000 B.C. the Emperor Huang-Ty had all available knowledge systematized in a Medical Encyclopedia, which was followed by a host of medico-philosophical treatises such as *The Mirror of Medicine, The Canon of the Yellow Pavilion,* and *The Canon of Wang-Hai-Tei.* The summary of the last-mentioned work given in Dr. Eugene Vincent's *Twentieth-Century Chinese Medicine* affords us some notion of the spirit of these compilations:

"The root of the negative soul is lodged in the 'brilliant star' (skull). The skull is formed by two doors: the 'door of heaven' (frontal parietal region) and the 'old door' (occipital region). On each side are two keys: the 'gilded key' (inner ear) and the 'jade key' (outer ear). The negative soul is in touch with the 'jade chamber' (chest), which contains the 'jade pearl' (heart) and the two 'suspended pearls' (lungs).

"The 'intermediate center' (seat of the involuntary actions) is in the abdomen, which is called the 'brilliant room' because it contains the 'solar organ' (liver), the 'lunar organ' (spleen), and the six 'luminous junctions' (intestines).

"The 'lower center' or genitals (seat of the vital principle) is in the 'red palace,' which contains the 'mystery of spring' (uterus) in the woman and the 'two divine principles' in the man."

To this, Taoism, which regards sobriety as a factor of longevity, has added among other things the *Kuei Fa Yao Ping,* a treatise on prophylactic and curative medication of which the following is a summary given by Dr. Vincent:

"Chapter I deals with such fruits as the peach, banana and pineapple that regulate the vital heat of the intestines, fix the spirits, drive out malignant vapors, stop palpitations, prevent obstruction of the viscera and maintain the male spirit.

"Chapter II deals with such fruits as the melon, cucumber, orange, lemon, pomegranate, mango and mangosteen, which have the property of cleaning the intestines, relieving congestion of the viscera and purifying the urine.

"Chapter III deals with medlars, walnuts, almonds and other oily fruits which relieve constipation and are excellent remedies against 'excesses of the male principle' (the medlar is a sovereign remedy against venereal diseases and impurities of the blood).

"Chapter IV deals with the action of the doctor, who should look into the following four matters: the state of the circulation and of the humors (on the basis of pulsations), the state of respiration (indicated by the color of the face, lips, nostrils and eyes), the state of the viscera (on the basis of the color of the tongue, ears and skin of the stomach) and the state of the 'ascending and descending' humors (indicated by the sound of the voice and by the gaze). . . . This is almost a replica of Hippocratic medicine.

"Chapter V is concerned with treatment. First, absolute dieting in order to effect the *ching* (cleaning). Then, *kui-tsai* (vegetable diet), plus the fruits indicated earlier, and herb-teas. Tea, in particular, has the special property of effecting the *chang*. That is, of 'regularizing the ascending and descending currents of the humor' and of clarifying the sight."

When you have a fine Chinese dinner—which is very expensive, owing to the variety of ingredients required (swallow's-nests are more expensive than caviar)—you are therefore conforming, without being aware of it, to a semi-magical system of hygiene and therapy. Some of the dishes are meant to "heat the vital instincts," others to "freshen the humors." Shark's fins are for "long life." Coxcombs are for sexual potency. You also have aphrodisiacs, such as cloves, ginseng, crushed testicles of animals mixed with rice alcohol, soft staghorns, cantharides —and also anaphrodisiacs such as water-lily root, ginger, and Japanese spindle bark. Furthermore, Cholon is full of herbalist shops, which look rather like wizards' or alchemists' dens with their products steeping in jars and their medicinal roots tied in bunches and hanging from the ceiling.

With regard to homeopathy—which is also known to the Chinese—I should like to give a current recipe for disintoxicating opium addicts:

"Ginseng, miscellaneous herbs, and a quantity of opium pellets corresponding to the patient's state of opium poisoning are placed in a bottle three-quarters full of Cinzano. The mixture is allowed to steep. The patient is then given two spoonfuls of the product. This quantity is replaced by an equal quantity of pure Cinzano. Thus, the strength of the mixture and the opium content are progressively reduced until the bottle no longer contains any opium at all. Disintoxication is carried out as gently as can be."

XIV

I ALSO paid a visit to an astrologer to see how he operated and whether what he said would confirm or contradict what I had been told by Western astrologers who had cast my horoscope.

We found him in the familiar setting of a room which contained the altar of the ancestors and which opened directly onto the street. He was a bright-looking man. Although our visit was unannounced, he declared himself to be delighted. Whether he was being sincere or simply polite, the fact is that you will never see a Chinese look annoyed if you drop in on him unexpectedly. (One can imagine the reaction of a Western "specialist" to such behavior.)

He first served us tea in tiny cups, in the Northern manner. Then, when my friend, after a reasonable lapse of time, informed him of the purpose of my visit, he laughed amiably. However, as soon as I told him the day and hour of my birth he changed his tone and got down to work. First he picked up a Chinese calendar in order to make the necessary conversion. Then he assembled the material he needed to write the characters.

I am always fascinated when I see a Chinese writing. It is no casual act that he is performing, for it requires a whole preparation, first ritual and then internal, before the first character appears under the brush. "Writing," says Yang Yu-shun, "is regarded in China as one of the higher forms of art. It therefore requires careful preparation. The bristles should be those of a hare that has been caught on a mountaintop in August or September. . . . For poems, the finest quality is necessary. In writing his preface to the *Miscellany of the Orchid Pavilion,* the great calligrapher Wang Hi-tche used a brush tipped with the whiskers of mice."

"To crush the ink-stick on stone," says the *Han Lin Yao Kiue,* "press hard against the stone and push gently. In making a wide detour you go farther. You then bring it back by a small detour. Therein lies the true secret." In the holding of the brush, each finger plays a particular role. The position of the wrist and arm are also of prime importance, for the "vital flux" must be smooth. "Writing," says Chiang Lee in his *Chinese Calligraphy,* "is an adventure in movement. Movement is the very breath of our calligraphy. Two kinds of movement are distinguished. The first may be called 'activity in stillness,' the second 'activity in action.' . . . The brush may be likened to the bow and arrow. When an archer has thoroughly sighted his target, poised his body, grasped his bow firmly and aimed accurately, the arrow will certainly hit the mark. So with the calligrapher. . . . Never try to write until you have calmed yourself completely. Any sort of rush before writing is fatal."

These, more or less, were the preparations of the astrologer as I witnessed them. First he concentrated, with his eyes half closed; then he gathered his vital spirits. Having done this, he repressed, in accordance with the Tao, the twenty-four dispositions (the six appetites, six hindrances, six sentiments, and six attitudes) in order to achieve emptiness and illumination. Vision and audition must not linger over any particular object. In order for the perception to be pure, it must be *diffuse,* must relate to the whole and not to details. "The true sage," says Lie-tse, "hears with his eyes and sees with his ears. It matters not whether he perceives through his ears or four limbs, or whether it is through his heart, stomach, or five viscera that he is informed." And regarding concentration, Tchuang-tse declares: "Do you want to be a good archer? Spend two years lying under your wife's loom, and when the spindle grazes your eyes, force yourself not to blink. Then, for three years spend all your time making a louse climb up a silken thread, contemplating it all the while with your face to the light. When the louse seems larger than a wheel, when it seems larger than a mountain, it will hide the sun from you. When you see its heart, then take your bow and shoot boldly. You will hit the louse in the center of its heart without even grazing the silken thread." [1]

Suddenly, with almost violent vigor, the astrologer began to draw signs on the white sheet. Every now and then he would stop, the better to receive the communication, and then resume his stroking. When the sheet was covered with signs the astrologer paused, reflected, then

[1] Quoted by Granet in *Chinese Thought.*

rapidly linked up certain signs in order to establish the "correspondences."

Finally he looked up, smiled, and made some observations which my friend interpreted approximately. What he said excited me, for though he had come to the same conclusions as the Western astrologers, he had reached them by an entirely different route. He said, for example: "The eight characters are favorable. Therefore, there is nothing intrinsically bad. Six characters out of eight are *yang*. Thus, the *yang* predominates. But the element 'Earth' is too prominent. That creates an imperfect balance. The element 'Fire' is lacking [for the Chinese, fire is an emollient]." He then began to paint my character as if I were utterly transparent.

At last he stopped. I waited a moment. Then, through the interpreter, I asked him what he thought from the point of view of physiognomy.

He raised his eyes and studied me. Suddenly he burst into laughter, as if he had just noticed something prodigiously amusing. Then, just as suddenly, he shut up like a clam. In a second he was talking of something else: he was offering my friend a concubine!

What was it that could have caused the astrologer's outburst and then his sudden silence? I left his home considerably intrigued, as one can imagine. Had he seen something fatal in me?

"We'll know one day," said my friend as we walked off. "Only you musn't be in a hurry."

I made up my mind that I would visit the astrologer again in order to get to the bottom of the matter. But events, unhappily, willed otherwise.

XV

MISS FOM LIN-FAN was playing at the Dai La Tien Theater during my stay. I made it my business to see her, for she was regarded as the leading Chinese operetta star, owing to her exquisite femininity and her voice. The Chinese attach great importance to the "tone" of the voice, going so far as to make notations of the first bawlings of a newborn babe in order to have some inkling of his future character. Miss Fom Lin-fan's voice was recognized by her countrymen as the ultimate in purity. Of course, the modulations of Chinese voices are difficult for the Western ear to become accustomed to. As for myself, I must admit that the Chinese music which was bawled out so generously at the Sun Wah had sounded to me at first like caterwauling and had put me into such a state that I felt as if my nerve ends were being tickled with feathers. And then, little by little, I reached a point at which hearing it, after a few hours of abstinence, had become a need, like the slaking of thirst. The reader will therefore understand the eagerness with which I accepted the invitation to hear Miss Fom Lin-fan.

Once again I found myself, owing to Chinese politeness, in the first row of the orchestra—a politeness all the more meaningful in that tickets were at a premium. Miss Fom Lin-fan's coming had created a black market, all seats having been immediately bought up by speculators and resold at more than double their price. Can one imagine a Parisian worker shelling out fifty dollars to take his wife and two kids to hear *Pelléas and Mélisande?* For the Chinese of all classes, the theater is an education, and they revere their actors, whom they regard not only as masters of form but as possessors of a semi-magical power.

If I speak of "reverence" in connection with Chinese actors, I do so because they are not only brought up in the theater—as the bonzes are in the pagoda—but because they form a "congregation" apart. They live very strictly among themselves, even when not performing, and they are thoroughly absorbed in their profession, particularly as, according to Chinese belief, there is a mysterious relationship between the performer and the various characters he embodies. Certain roles are even regarded as so dangerous, because of the baleful influence they transmit to those who play them, that they may not be performed unless the actor has taken the greatest precautions. This makes it necessary for each troupe to place itself under the protection of particular divinities (as indicated by the streamer above the curtain) and to precede each performance with propitiatory rites.

I have already pointed out that the theater is not only an entertainment but a school of manners. You learn how to win a woman who is beyond reach, how to get out of a delicate situation gracefully. The Chinese drama is rich in comedies of manners wherein subtlety vies with shrewdness—two qualities particularly dear to the Chinese. Despite the fact that the audience knows the repertory by heart, what they come to see particularly is the actor's personal style. To be sure, gestures in the Chinese theater are subject to extremely strict rules. A certain movement of the wrist expresses a particular feeling; a given gesture with a fan means something else. But rules do not interfere with individual style. The grandeur of the Chinese theater—as of Chinese life— arises from the fact that within the framework of conventions the individual who knows what he is about has the utmost freedom. The conflict between the artist and the rules exists no more here than it does for the matador in the bull ring. In bullfighting, each pass must, of course, be executed in a certain way, but that did not prevent Joselito and Belmonte, the two great rivals, from performing in quite different manners. It was precisely their personal styles that the *aficionados* of the period went to see, just as Frenchmen used to go to the Comédie Française to see Sarah Bernhardt and Réjane in the same role.

It was precisely this that the people came to see in Miss Fom Lin-fan. No sooner did she begin to perform than it was clear that she excelled the others. Not only, as far as I could judge, were the modulations of her voice extraordinarily pure, but she moved throughout the play, the plot of which grew increasingly complex, with the ease of a cat, and also with something of the feline's disturbing smoothness. Although she did not have the shapeliness of certain actresses, she was, more than any of them, an incarnation of feminine artfulness.

I know nothing more suggestive of sly desire, disguised concupiscence, or the feigned indifference of two people who want each other but hide their game as much as possible than the gestures employed in the Chinese theater. Each gesture is an achievement in itself. And if the performer sometimes takes a full minute to purse his lips in a certain way, to the accompaniment of a certain movement of the wrist, he does so because the subtlety of the feeling he depicts depends on the perfection of the gesture.

In the courtship scene, for example, the actor expressed, by his gaze alone, the various feelings that ran through him. And also by his long sleeves, which concealed his hands. The play of the sleeves was amazing. It lit up every shade of desire, every step in the progress of the conquest. They would grow bold, take on greater amplitude, describe, with great arabesques, the violence of desire. Then, when the fair one seemed startled, they would hastily retreat and close over the suitor, enveloping him without transition in the most complete humility. And meanwhile, Miss Fom Lin-fan would simper and twist her neck. She would play artfully with her handkerchief (at times hiding part of her face so as to conceal her emotion, at times shaking it haughtily to give vent to her wrath, or else, with the utmost delicacy, would dab her eyes with it to feign the approach of tears).

And as for costumes! Not only did the actors frequently have to change them several times in the course of an act, but they also had to change wigs and the numerous ornaments over their wigs. I can still see the incredible work Miss Fom Lin-fan had to do when I went to see her backstage between two appearances.

The wings, which were just behind the stage, were simply a long corridor, crowded with huge trunks, the kind used by actors the world over, but of shiny leather adorned with Chinese characters, and trestles on which were laid out some of the costumes. Other costumes, the more ornate ones, hung from the low ceiling and made the entire scene seem like something out of a museum of the emperors of China. What with the sumptuous bric-a-brac strewn all about, the effect bordered on the fantastic. I no longer felt I was backstage, but rather as if I were wandering about in a Chinese dream à la Walt Disney.

In the middle was a passageway so narrow that I had to lower my head to avoid the costumes, and when I raised it, I found myself face to face with a mandarin wearing a long beard, a horned headgear, a belt a span wide that girdled his waist aristocratically, and red leather boots with huge felt soles. Smiling amiably, he stepped aside to let me pass.

The actors' dressing rooms were simple cubicles separated from the corridor by a half-drawn curtain, so that I could see, as I glanced about, a "noble father" donning, with the help of three assistants, his ornament-laden costume, and, in the neighboring cubicle, the juvenile lead stretched out half naked on a camp chair and reviewing his script. His casual attire was explained by the fact that in order to prevent the perspiration from tarnishing the gilt of the costume the actor is obliged to wear underneath it a padded jacket that resembles a fencing plastron, for the actor drips with sweat while performing and has to be sponged as soon as he goes offstage.

Miss Fom Lin-fan, star that she was, was also separated from the rest only by a curtain. "All you need do," I was told, "is lift the curtain!" How free and easy it all was, considering the fact that she was the greatest actress of all China. And the good grace with which Miss Fom Lin-fan welcomed the anonymous Man of the West was in keeping with the rest. As she was unable to divert her attention from her preparations, she invited me with a smile to sit down . . . on one of her trunks. And without more ado she continued inspecting her face.

The actual making-up was only the beginning of the preparations. On Miss Fom Lin-fan's dressing table were, among other objects, a number of brown strips, very pointed at the ends and so shiny that I thought at first they were made of cardboard. But they were real hair glued together into locks of various lengths. When she finished her actual make-up, Miss Fom Lin-fan took these locks one after the other, starting with the shortest, and, using fish paste, made herself a set of bangs, the longest of the locks going behind her ear and down to her chin.

When she had done this, the wardrobe mistress, who was like wardrobe mistresses the world over, set on her head a wig, also made of actual hair, and a long braid.

There still remained the headgear, a perforated diadem with pendants. The adjusting of this accessory was a job in itself, for the diadem was composed of detached parts which had to be adjusted one by one, each being joined to the other.

All of this, added to the broad-sleeved, gold-embroidered costume, the shoulders of which were, in addition, encrusted with precious stones, now gave Miss Fom Lin-fan a quite other bearing. Before my very eyes she had plunged backward into time and entered the realm of legend. The human face of a moment before had disappeared; in its place was a mysterious and hieratic figure.

XVI

THOUGH the theater is one of the places where the Chinese spirit reveals itself most particularly, it does so even more singularly in the pagoda. Not long after my arrival I was advised by a Cholon scholar to visit one of these temples. "That's where all Chinese life has its source," he said. "But don't go to the pagodas simply out of idle curiosity. If you do, you won't learn a thing. Live in them! Stay for hours on end until you steep yourself in the atmosphere. Since time immemorial, the pagoda has been the center of the community. It is the place where the Chinese makes fresh contact with his origins. It is also a rallying place. Women go there—in fact the pagoda is frequented only by women—not only to carry out their rites but also, as you will see, to merge with the others in the community atmosphere that distinguishes Chinese life."

There are various types of pagoda in Cholon, each attended by its local congregation. The need to get together in groups is particularly strong, owing to the fact that, though Cholon was founded one hundred and eighty years ago, its inhabitants are nevertheless emigrants. Those whose forebears were from Canton gather around the Cantonese Pagoda. Others frequent the Pagoda of the Jade Emperor or the Monastery of the Crimson Bamboo Forest, depending on whether they are Confucians, Buddhists, or Taoists, although there is no sharp separation or rivalry among these three "persuasions." None of these concepts—for they are not so much religions, as we understand the word, as concepts—is exclusive. Such exclusiveness would be contrary to the Chinese mentality. Nor is any one of them imperative. It merely indicates "recipes." Each individual freely chooses from among these concepts the one that seems to him most efficacious. And the Chinese, circumspect man that he is, is quite ready to dip into all three of them. As a friend once said to me, and very rightly, "To ask a Chinese what his religion is, is meaningless. Generally speaking, one might say that every Chinese is a bit of a Confucian, a bit of a Taoist, and a bit of a Buddhist."

As the Cantonese Pagoda drew a larger crowd than any of the others, that was the one I went to most often. Besides, the atmosphere there was more familiar. The Cantonese Pagoda is a huge building next door to the large Cantonese school (3000 pupils), which it supports financially.

The door, which is open all day long, opens into a kind of colonnaded hall with, on one side, a statue of the tutelary god in a niche, and, on the other, that of the Mandarin of the Gate. Beyond the entrance hall is a long unroofed "patio" around which runs a kind of cloister that contains benches for the visitors and tables for the bonzes and priestesses who interpret the fates. A partition of wonderfully intricate fretwork separates this first patio from a second, which is somewhat more closed off than the other and at the far end of which the Lady of the Place sits in state: "The Mother (A-fo), also known as the Celestial Empress." She is flanked by two "aides": on the right, the Dragon Queen; on the left, the Lady with the Golden Flower. The figures are placed in an area of semidarkness which sets off the gold of the statues, the copper of the urns—huge receptacles with heavy handles—and the chasing of the gigantic perfume braziers.

The effect of it all is that of a magical den, both sumptuous and disquieting, a kind of Madame Tussaud's display of the Other World, for each of the divinities, whether of gold, bronze, or dark wood, is adorned, like the Great Ones of the Earth, with rich costumes, oddly shaped headgear, and, depending on the status of each, boots, bootees, or thick felt slippers. And each has not only his wardrobe—which is solemnly renewed every year—but also his food. Each is surrounded with choice viands—chicken smeared with honey, bowls of rice, plates of fruit—which are constantly renewed so that he can satisfy his appetite at any moment. It is necessary to indulge the divinities in order to maintain them in a state of euphoria. . . . Thus, in the neighboring pagoda there is a stone tiger who is forever being gorged with fat and blood, which can be bought at the door. Part of the food is put into his mouth and the rest is set before him (it is all immediately removed by the attendants in order to make way for the next offering). Elsewhere is a horse, a wooden horse, who is offered hay. To avoid disturbing him, the faithful slip it between his teeth. All this is done with the utmost seriousness, as if the celestial personages were human beings.

The last time I went to the Cantonese Pagoda, I found a dense throng in front of the entrance. Outside the temple, perched on a platform, was an orchestra of violins, flutes, and cymbals playing a frenzied and throbbing kind of music. It was the great annual holy day of the Cantonese, the festival of the Mother. Inside, the temple was teeming with women, each busy with her devotions, all of them dressed alike in black and with their braids very neatly plaited. Unlike the ceremonies in our places of worship, where, however many people are present, the rites are the same for all, here everyone was busy with her own personal rite.

One would be standing before a huge counter fitted out with whatever was needed for every possible kind of supplication, buying a package of sticks of incense that she would then light one by one and place at the four corners of the pagoda; or she might set a sheaf of them before a particular divinity. Another would take two pieces of crescent-shaped sandalwood, flat on one side and convex on the other, and, after making the ritual bows in the direction of the four azimuths, would throw them to the floor, pick them up, then throw them down again to see whether the gods were favorable to her and whether there were a chance of her invocation's being heeded. It was necessary that one piece fall on the flat surface and the other on the convex. She would then question the fates with the aid of the divining rods. To do so she would take up a bamboo cylinder containing 101 such rods (thin, flat stems, each bearing a different inscription) and, facing the divinity whose aid she was beseeching, would shake the cylinder violently until one rod emerged from the set. Then she would carry it to one of the bonzes sitting at the entrance. The bonze would open a book to find the reference indicated on the rod and would read the oracle, in a monotone, as if his mind were far away, like our own clairvoyants when they deliver their messages.

Elsewhere, a petitioner, kneeling on the flagstones in front of a particular divinity, would be assisted by an attendant who would read for her the ritual supplication, breaking off from time to time to grasp her by the back of the neck and strike her head roughly on the stones. In another spot, a woman would present to the bonze a child she was carrying in her arms, and the monk, holding a square piece of paper mounted on bamboo—its form resembled that of a kite—would utter some cabalistic words which were intended to deliver the youngster from the evil that possessed him. Whereupon, with a rapid movement, he would push the frame against the child's body, thereby ripping the paper, so that the child would cross the "threshold" between illness and health.

But these were all ordinary rites, such as are performed throughout the year, as need arises. The extraordinary feature of the festival of the Mother lies in the offerings. On this occasion the most sumptuous gifts are offered in order to ensure oneself of her protection during the year to come. And the spectacle is veritably awe-inspiring! Lining the cloister are more than a hundred images of divinities, all of them far larger than life, set side by side in fantastic display, a hundred human representations of the celestial divinities, entirely made of paper and glued to a framework of bamboo slats, but all so artfully cut out that you would swear they were spangled and brocaded, set with emeralds and rubies and diamonds, and not merely objects of glazed paper. Chinese mythology looms before you in all its grandeur, each figure representing a different divinity: the God of Fertility, the God of Honors, the God of Riches or Prosperity or Justice. And each with its particular attributes, one with a round headgear, another with a square one, to which were attached earlike loops, a third with high boots made of handsome red leather (at least, one would swear they are), a fourth with pointed fur-lined bootees; and all wear richly embroidered cloaks. They stand before you rigid and solemn. But what is most astonishing in this Carnival of the Other World is that everything becomes alive. Rigid though they be, these figures *live,* with a fantastic kind of life. Never had I seen inert objects that had such vitality, save, perhaps, the recumbent figures in the Church of St. Denis, the slumbering kings and queens whom one expects at any moment to awaken.

All along this fantastic gallery—which recalls the armor rooms of our museums—the women came and went with the diligence of ants, each preoccupied with her own tasks. But unlike our religious gatherings, or those in India, where the soul of the crowd is collective, each woman went about her own business, unconcerned with the others, in somewhat the same way customers in a department store during a bargain sale worm their

way through the mob single-mindedly toward a particular goal. If such a comparison occurs to me so readily, it
does so because there is no exaltation, no fervor at the
pagoda. The Chinese temperament, though it may be
poetic or spiritualistic, is not at all mystical.

The Chinese lives as familiarly as can be with the
Spirits of the Other World. Thus, on certain days of the
year, he leaves on his doorstep rice and other food for
the Threshold God or carefully places at the curb of the
sidewalk—quite regardless of the flow of traffic—sticks
of incense and a small bouquet of flowers to appease the
Wandering Souls. The impression is that of simple routine. Commerce with the Spirits is carried out in accordance with a system that has proved effective over
thousands of years and whose rules must be observed
without a slip.

Outside the temple the orchestra kept playing away
in order to give pleasure to the ears of the divinities;
inside, the same function was performed by gongs, placed
in strategic spots. And whenever a petitioner reached
the climax of her rite—which she carried out in hot
haste, lest, were she to pause for even a few seconds, the
god turn his head elsewhere—a gong was struck to attract the attention of the High Official of the Afterlife,
to the accompaniment of a "Huh, huh!" uttered by the
bonze as if to say: "You're being called. Do you hear?
Look, you're being offered a very fine gift!" It reminded
me of the *Olé!* with which Spaniards rekindle a waning
fervor.

The ceremonies went on uninterruptedly for three
days, three days of seething and swarming and of more
or less sumptuous offerings, depending on the individual's

"*Thus, all the paper gods were set afire one after the other and carried, still flaming, to the huge urns intended for receiving the ashes. All that remained was a procession of women bearing torches and moving towards one or the other crematorium, with flames darting forth on all sides.*"

means. On the last day, when all was over, everything was burned. The whole wonderful setting went up in a great auto-da-fée, by reason of the Chinese belief that the mere fact of burning an object, whatever it be, confers magical power upon it. For example, the Chinese are careful never to throw out even the most casual piece of writing. It has to be burned. And there are special pagodas, known as "pagodas of compassion for characters," which receive the ashes. Moreover, persons who are sentenced to death are never burned alive for fear of the force they may acquire.

Thus all the paper gods were set afire one after the other and carried, still flaming, to the huge urns intended for receiving the ashes. All that remained was a procession of women bearing torches and moving toward one or the other crematorium, with flames darting forth on all sides.

Finally everything was in ashes. Despite the open sky, the atmosphere was heavy with incense and burned paper and was almost unbreathable. The festival was over. The pagoda had done a flourishing business, and the Chinese were at peace, having satisfied their gods for another year.

XVII

I Became increasingly aware, during my stay, of the importance of woman in Chinese society as officiant and guardian of the religious tradition. My personal observations in this respect were confirmed and supplemented by what I was told by European friends who were married to Chinese women.

With reference to the "status of woman" in the world, I see, roughly speaking, four distinct states. There is that of woman in so-called primitive societies. The man is the unchallenged master. For the most part the woman is not consulted. She simply obeys. Her only defense is guile, for she is generally shrewder than the man and, however submissive she may appear to be, always achieves her ends. She hints and suggests, and, in the end, leads the man by the nose, though letting him think that it is he who has taken the initiative.

Then there is the Western woman, of whom the Frenchwoman seems to me the most highly evolved type. She is neither a slave nor a completely free agent, but combines the activities of the two, though without performing a well-defined role in the marital relationship.

Then there is the American, the emancipated woman, who often practices a profession and has the same status as the man. She has her own checkbook, takes part in politics, and is, in short, the man's equal—often his superior. In America, male and female are no longer complementary. Often they are rivals. Woman has, if I may say so, invaded man's domain. In doing so, she has gradually lost her status as woman; she loses her sexual attractiveness to the degree that she discards her femininity in the effort to attain what can only be called, psychologically speaking, of course, and not physiologically, a hybrid state. The woman has lifted herself out of the state of submission. She has, if you like, won out. But her victory is a tragic one, for she is in conflict with her essential nature.

Let us turn to the Chinese woman. Her state seems to me to be the most harmonious of all. She is neither the man's slave nor his rival. Husband and wife play a specific role, and neither infringes on the other's. Each has his and her domain and prerogatives, and neither is superior to the other. There is thus a balance, and it is the maintenance of this balance and the precise definition of roles that seem to me so remarkable in the Chinese family. The woman is the mistress of the home. It is she who commands there and who brings up the children.

I was once told by a Chinese, a man eminently respectful of tradition, "Since it is she who is in charge of rearing my children, I never make the slightest criticism

"In China the woman is neither the man's slave nor his rival . . ."

"The Chinese woman is the mistress of the home; it is she who commands there and who brings up the children."

of any of them except through their mother. It is she who
must make the comment, not I. And that is only just. If
my wife has any remarks to make about *my* work, she
does so only with the utmost tact. I owe her the same
consideration in regard to hers. It is she who is the
guardian of the home, and not I. And there is no conflict
between us. I have been in Europe," he continued,
"where on occasion I have heard such remarks as 'mind
your own business.' Such words are never uttered among
us. If they were, it would mean that the structure of the
home had been destroyed. I pray to the gods that such
a thing may never happen!"

Of course it may seem odd that in Cholon the Chinese
never "takes his wife out," except to dine with friends.
Is this subservience what some persons might consider an
"outrageous maintenance of the state of inferiority"? I
do not think so. Here the woman simply confines herself
to her role. Except when she goes to visit women friends,
she remains at home, in *her* domain. Therein, as it seems
to me, lies the strength of the Chinese framework. Within
this framework each feels perfectly free and independent.
How independent, for example, were the boyesses of my
hotel, including the old woman who cleaned my room!
"This is *my* hour," she seemed to say each time she
entered. She would take over like a pilot who assumes
command of a vessel when it enters port and who, as
soon as he sets foot on the bridge, is lord and master of
the ship and knows exactly what to do. In like manner,
the Chinese woman is imbued with her role. This gives
her an extraordinarily compact quality.

Take the Chinese girl as she walks through the street
with her peculiarly fluid movement. However thin she

is, she never seems frail. Her body is firm and supple, with the elasticity of the frog. Indeed, the body of the Chinese woman, with its drooping shoulders, long, thin bust, and swelled-out hips, curiously suggests the frog. But this thinness is "full."

And what poise she has! How different from the Vietnamese girl, who preens herself in the street. She smiles and leads you on. The Chinese girl does nothing to arouse you. At most, you may catch a gleam in her eye, a gleam that issues from her depths. As she goes by, she seems to have a definite goal, whereas you feel the Vietnamese girl is aimless, fickle-minded, not disinclined to lead men on. The Chinese girl does not lead you on, but if she wants you she can be exquisitely subtle.

I discussed Chinese women with P_____. How P_____ came to China is an odd story in itself. His father had been a painter, a fairly good portrait painter, without great talent and without success. One day a client appeared and asked to have his portrait painted. The artist set to work. The result was satisfactory. The client then revealed his identity. He was the Minister of Finance. He said to the painter, "Rather than pay you in money, I'm going to give you some stock-market tips. Follow them, and you'll be a rich man." The painter did not need to be urged. He invested the little money he had. The investment paid off. Investments followed in quick succession. The man was transformed. The obscure artist was now a speculator. Money kept rolling in. He became a fashionable figure . . . and then the scandal broke. Before he knew what it was all about, he found himself liable to imprisonment. The gentleman in him thereupon awoke. He committed suicide, leaving behind

a son without a penny and with a blemished name. The
boy had been planning to go to the Naval Academy,
but he no longer had the means; besides, he would have
felt uncomfortable there. Choosing a second-best solution, he entered the Naval Engineering School. As he
was—with good reason—uncommunicative, the others
hazed him. He withdrew more deeply into himself.
Happily, the sailor's trade led him far from home.
Eventually his ship took him to China. Everywhere else
he had encountered rudeness and brutality, but there
nobody was rude to anyone. People were polite and
affable. They did not discourage his approach. He
married a Chinese woman. Not that this happened overnight. But the Chinese are great hands at taming men
as well as birds. They tamed P_____. What he would
not have done by himself, they did for him. They charmed
him.

He came to see me at the Sun Wah. I asked him, "Are
you happy with your wife?"

His face lit up. "As happy as a man could be! There's
never any problem with her. There's never a loud word,
never any argument. I can't imagine a better companion." He had just sent her to Europe to make the acquaintance of his family.

"Do you think they'll hit it off?" I asked. I could
hardly imagine a French provincial town welcoming her
very enthusiastically.

P_____ shrugged his shoulders. "Some of them will
probably pull a long face, those for whom the Chinese
mean only 'the yellow race.' But before long they'll be
eating out of her hand."

P_____ was not the only one who spoke to me in

that vein. Others had said the same kind of thing, exactly the same. Yet not all of them were easy persons to get on with. For example, B_____. B_____ was a former sailor in the Navy who had moved over, some time before, to the merchant marine. He looked like a real "bruiser" and was built like an icebox, with the mug of a boxer—he had once been a boxing champion—and a completely flattened nose, though his eyes were as blue as a child's. A tender brute, that's what he was, the kind of person with whom you click right away or never.

We went strolling about town. When we sat down at the terrace of a café, we began speaking about the Chinese woman. How B_____ happened to be married to one was quite a story. B_____ had, when very young, been married, in France, to a girl with whom he had been violently in love. But while he was at sea someone had taken her from him. Had it been a man, B_____ would have smashed his jaw. He could have handled anyone. But the someone happened to be a woman. And she had taken his wife from him for good. What irony! The colossus had been done in by a lesbian.

B_____ went away, never to return. He went wherever there was fighting, like a man running away from himself. He was at Saigon when Frenchmen were being murdered there. "All I had on me was a pocket knife. But by means of the knife I managed to get hold of a revolver. After that, things were easy." I did not ask for details about the "after that." It might have been tactless. Besides, B———was not very loquacious. But when I began speaking about Chinese women he livened up. He was the kind of man in whom you have to touch the right chord, and who, once you do, talks on and on, particularly as most of the time he is taciturn.

Hearing him talk so volubly and forcibly, as had P_____, about the qualities of the Chinese woman, I wondered to myself, "Is this the bias of those who, having chosen to cast their lot with a race different from their own, have nothing but praise for what they've chosen?" But B_____ cared not a rap what race a person belonged to. He knew only individuals. As for women, he had knocked about the world a long time and, male that he was, had had them in every corner of the globe. If someone had "nailed" him, she must have had something that the others had lacked. For B_____ was not a man to get involved, not the sort of man who could be tied down or with whom a woman could stage a scene. That kind of thing would not have lasted long with him. A slap on the face and out she'd go.

Yet a Chinese woman had got him. And she had him good and proper. "I can't even imagine," he said, "the slightest misunderstanding between her and me. And as for agreeableness and charm, she displays more in one day than any European woman does in ten years!"

I heard the same refrain elsewhere, in almost identical terms. Obviously marriage is peculiarly meaningful for the Chinese, and I think I understand the reason why. The basis on which it rests is exceptionally firm and deep-rooted. There too I recognize Chinese wisdom, which, seeing man not from the point of view of the ideal, but *as he is,* has therefore sought in marriage the most "functional" solution. I have already spoken of how the marriage partner is chosen in China. Not on the basis of a hasty impulse, even less on that of passion, which is considered dangerous, for it is blind and short-lived, but on the infinitely more solid basis of deep affinities. I have described the care with which parents go about selecting a prospective bride for their sons, how they consult diviners in order to know to what extent the girl's eight characters harmonize with those of her future spouse, and to determine whether the five elements, the ancestral heredity, and the year of birth are compatible with those of the future partner. I have also pointed out that the head of the family (who is the representative on earth of the ancestors and whose duty it is, as such, to see to it that no baleful influence disturbs the ancestral flux, which, flowing through the ages, means, for the Chinese, eternity) acts on such occasions as the supreme judge of the future welfare of his son. The introduction of a foreign element into the family cell has implications that are too far-reaching to be lightly undertaken. Everything must be properly examined. Chinese marriage is somewhat like our old-time "marriage of reason." I can still recall, from the time of my childhood, the minuteness with which the families inquired, without the knowledge of the future bride and groom, into the antecedents of each, his and her breeding, sense of values, health, and character. These questions were the subject of an intensive epistolary exchange, not directly with the parents (lest one lose face in the event of a refusal—we too were somewhat Chinese), but with relatives "in a good position to know." However, despite these precautions, the marriages were not always successful.

The Chinese loathe discord. Chinese marriage seems

to be something better than a "marriage of reason"; it is one of "wisdom." They do not aim at an unattainable ideal. With their characteristic common sense, the Chinese see man as he is. If the husband ceases to find his wife sexually attractive, it is up to her to find him promptly a pretty girl who will satisfy him and to set her up in the home as a concubine. The "legitimate" wife does not lose face, since it is she who instigates the act. She is aware of everything that is happening, since her husband's mistress is right in her own home. And it is the wife who is in charge. Far from being reduced, her prestige is increased by the presence of an additional member of the household. Not only does she remain the unchallenged mistress of the home, but the children her husband has by the concubine are under her supervision, exactly as are her own children. How much better this is for the general equilibrium and the preservation of the cell than the solutions of Western peoples! How much preferable, to my way of thinking, to American divorce or the European "triangle" that, in the last analysis, leaves everyone unsatisfied, to say nothing of the humiliation of the deceived partner. Some persons may regard the Chinese solution as amoral. To this the Chinese would reply, "Do you regard as 'moral' the liaison that wounds people or the divorce that shatters everything? We Chinese destroy nothing, or as little as possible." Marriage in China is not, as in America, a provisional association that breaks up as soon as it ceases to be satisfactory. Nor is it, as in Europe, a religious obligation, a commandment that is respected willy-nilly. It is a lifetime pact. It is, in fact, a threefold commitment: first, toward one's ancestors; secondly, toward the spouse; and thirdly, toward oneself. It is an imperative, not from without but from within.

That is no doubt why Chinese marriage holds up. It is based on unity. As my friends said to me, "It is when things go badly that the strength of the bond becomes apparent."

And B——— knew what that meant! "When I was taken prisoner by the Japanese," he said, "my wife came to see me every day to bring me food. God knows the insults she had to put up with because of that . . . to say nothing of an occasional whack with a rifle butt. Since the yellow men were winning, she might have felt that she belonged to them. But not at all. The fact that I had married her was the one and only consideration. That's where her loyalty lay. Can you see a white woman married to a Chinese doing the same thing?

"And it's not only my wife who is behind me. There are my in-laws, who treat me like a son. Whenever I go to see them, my slightest desire is fulfilled. And behind them there are the relatives and the friends. It's as if I married not only a Chinese woman but all of China!"

Regarding this sense of solidarity that constitutes the strength of the Chinese, B——— once said to me, "During the war I was passing with my cargo boat through the Straits of Formosa when a Japanese destroyer was amusing itself by sinking Chinese fishing junks. I managed to slip in and rescue Chinese sailors struggling in the water. After that I had free entrance to all the ports along the coast. Wherever I went there was always a cargo for me, even when there was none for anyone else. Wherever I turned up the people seemed to know me.

It's amazing how informed they are, though there's no knowing exactly how they get their information.

"And their information goes a long way. Years after the incident I've just related, I was shipwrecked near Aden with a Chinese crew. We swam to shore, having lost everything. Within an hour a Chinese introduced himself. 'I know who you are,' he said. 'What do you need?' "

XVIII

DOES what I have said mean that I have "understood" China? Any such pretension would be quite ridiculous. "It has taken me forty-five years," a missionary once said to me, "to understand the little I know about the country. And now that I've reached that point, I can no longer explain that little to those of my kind!" In order to understand China, one must, as do the Chinese, *perceive* the universe, and not understand it intellectually. But how can one expect a man who has had an abstract training to have a concrete view of things? How is one to reconcile our ethics with that of Lao-tse, who says, "I believe the truthful man; I also believe the liar," and who sees Good and Evil as simply two aspects of the same truth? For the Chinese, to comprehend means to incorporate a truth into oneself physically. How can we pretend to such perception, we who have departed from the state of nature and have lost the simplicity that the Chinese have preserved? How can we grasp the Tao and the "being of non-being," which recalls the anti-proton, whose existence in non-existence perplexes scientists?

I think of the definitions of the Tao that Marcel Granet has attempted to give in his *Chinese Thought:*

"According to Tchung-tse, 'There are no contrary terms; there are only contrasting appreciations. Complete changes are only mutations. . . . The only truths are those that are circumstantial, impermanent, multiple, individual, concrete, or, what amounts to the same, there is only *one* abstract total and independent truth, and that is the *Tao,* the *mean*—indifferent and neutral, unmoved, undetermined, supremely autonomous—of the ensemble of transitory truths, of the contrasting impressions, of the spontaneous mutations.' One enjoys in advanced age the freshness of a child when one has cast out of oneself first the world of men, then all external reality and finally the very idea of existence. One then obtains, in a diffuse light, which is that of daybreak, the vision of a solitary independence, with the result that past and present are annihilated and one enters into what is neither living nor dying. . . . One is united to that which penetrates everywhere. . . . One adheres to the *Tao.*

"Lao-tse says: 'In order for perception to be pure, it must be *diffuse* and relate itself to the whole of things and not to their detail. It must be *total* and must be provided not by one of the senses but by the entire being. . . . Vomit forth your intelligence.' All dogma is harmful. Look at nothing, hear nothing. Let your eyes see nothing, your ears hear nothing, your heart know nothing. . . . A good master does not bother to explain the details of the trade. He acts in such a fashion that the governing principle becomes apparent to the disciple. He who can do knows neither why nor how he does. He knows only that he succeeds and that when one thinks with all one's being of succeeding and succeeding only, one always succeeds."

These definitions of the Tao by Western scholars may be intelligible to us, but does that mean that the Tao is also "perceptible" to us?

"The notion of the Tao seems to approximate that of Mana. . . . For the disciples of Confucius, the art of the Tao embraces all knowledge. They see in the Tao the virtue characteristic of the cultivated man who . . . plumes himself on possessing no particular talent. The Tao is first and foremost the Way. The word *Tao* summons up the image of a way to be followed, of a direction to give to conduct. Tao signifies regulating power, effective order. The Tao is the central perfection, the center of equivalences and contrasts, of attractions and repulsions. The Tao is the sovereign order."

This vision of the universe is certainly very different from ours! To quote Granet again: "When the Chinese meditates on the course of things, he does not seek to determine the general or calculate the probable. He is eager to detect the furtive, the singular. . . . Instead of noting successions of phenomena, the Chinese registers alternations of aspect. He refuses to consider the idea of cause and effect." As Lin Yutang has said: "He knows only provisional opinions, momentary truths. . . . China's peculiar contribution to philosophy is the distrust of systematic philosophy. . . . The temperament for systematic philosophy simply isn't there, and will not be there so long as the Chinese remain Chinese."

The Chinese has no philosophical system, but he lives

philosophically, unlike us. "Does the West have a philosophy?" asks Lin Yutang. "The answer is clearly no. . . . We need a philosophy of living and we haven't got it. The Western man has tons of philosophy written by French, German, English and American professors. But still he hasn't got a philosophy when he wants it."

"In order to understand the first thing about China," I was told, "you must rid yourself of your Western concept." But this is more easily said than done. How difficult it is to imagine a logic other than our own!

Take the Chinese tradesman in whose shop a friend of mine found that rarest thing during the war: electric bulbs.

"What's the price of a bulb?"

"Sixty francs."

"All right. Give me a dozen."

"That will be a thousand francs."

"What? You just told me they cost sixty francs apiece!"

"Yes, but you're taking twelve. That means you need them badly. Every need has to be paid for."

Similarly, if a Chinese asks twice the value of an article, he is not being dishonest. He is simply challenging you. It's up to you to make a countermove. If you do not, not only will you be cheated, but you will lose the seller's respect. Is not this somewhat the attitude of our horse traders and antique dealers? Not to accept the game is to lose credit with the dealer—and with the Chinese dealer more than any other.

Although I lived amidst Chinese, they remained thoroughly foreign to me. I lived beside them, not with them. And smiling though they were, my contact with them left me with a feeling of strangeness, with the vague fear one has when one brushes against the unknown.

I had this sensation particularly at night, when the acetylene lamps of the street stalls cast strange gleams on faces and their sputtering seemed to express the very pulsation of the street. Things would dance before my eyes. Everything appeared to be moving, elusive. A white jacket, which was all that might be seen of a person, would float above the sidewalk. Or three Chinese would be seated about a table, each wearing a different mask, one looking like a moonfish, another like a skeleton, a third, whose features were shifty, like a rat. Each had his own enigmatic smile. Elsewhere a skeleton would lean against the trees. And the hands and long spatelike fingers seemed to reach out not only to take objects but to caress them.

There were also the odors that wafted through the air —hot fat that would make me nauseous, musk, ginseng, and all the spices that the Chinese use in their cooking. Or there would be the whiffs of opium. And the odor of perspiration. Near the Arroyo, it was the smell of rotting fish that predominated, mingled with that of slime and dung from the river. And everywhere were people, some sleeping on a simple mat or even right on the pavement, others strolling (the Chinese has a peculiar way of shuffling along, as if always on the alert), others eating. But everywhere life had a quality of force.

It is at night that the Chinese seems to be functioning most completely. And when he functions, he does so as if in heat. For him, being in heat is not peculiar to sexuality. He takes such intense delight in sheer living that this "heat" is in everything he does. It does not arise out of obscenity; obscenity does not exist for the Chinese. It is the result of sheer delight. And it imparts to the night a violent, exacerbated throbbing which, to the Westerner that I was, had a disturbing effect.

The reeking foods displayed all about in the stalls with the light playing on them, the fowl smeared with honey, the gizzards, the inner organs, were no longer mere foods, but something erotic. The passer-by was offered a culinary Garden of Caresses; he was being tempted to "achieve pleasure through visual stimulation." The Westerner, invited to partake of centipedes with flower of cinnamon, python soup, rose wine, dragon's eyes spiced with tiger's blood or salmi spangled with deer tongue, feels himself to be at the threshold of a new and mysterious world. He suddenly discovers unexpected possibilities in his organs, new kinds of eroticism in this hallucinating universe. Tortoise mouths, lizard claws, tongues of scorpions reach out to him. The bladders and gizzards, twisted and grotesque as the motifs on the roofs of the pagodas, seem to him less food than idols. The red and green and bronze-colored syrups shining in their jars, reminiscent of the display windows of our old-fashioned pharmacies, the bluish-green fermentations into which the cook dips his ladle to make mysterious mixtures, these smack of alchemy. Are they elixirs of long life? Are they aphrodisiacs?

The European is perplexed by this fertility of imagination, by what is almost lubricity in refinement. He feels new modes of being awakening within him. He senses, almost with terror, for he knows not where these new desires may lead him, a broadening of his being, a limitless extension of his possibilities. Everything tempts him in this spectacle of eroticism, and at the same time everything about the Chinese alarms him. To what other people in the world would it have occurred to let eggs rot for weeks on end in order to see the result of this maceration? Perhaps some subtle broth awakening strange appetites, awakening the urge not to lie with a girl but with a beardless boy or with a vixen (as mentioned in old Chinese texts).

Such things as these the Westerner discovers to his astonishment as he goes to live in a Chinese city. And he is offered not only the whole gamut of buccal eroticism that only the subtlest imagination can conceive, but all the sexual, opiated fantasies that the imagination of his body, suddenly liberated, may desire. Even before you have formulated the desire, a quest is under way. But there is no need to go far. Everything is within reach. The Chinese has foreseen everything, has explored all the possibilities of human desire. He is the alchemist of food, the master of aphrodisiacs, the man cunning in mixtures capable of producing within you strange mutations. He knows that there are rare affinities and rich concordances between living things. In his eyes there is nothing perverse, nothing obscene in this. Nothing is contrary to nature. If a thing *is,* it is thereby part of nature.

When the lamplights are finally extinguished, the magic ceases as at a given signal. The street hawker's trays are folded up. Within a few minutes everything is dismantled. Of the magicians' booths, made of a few boards and slats held together by string and covered with a simple awning, there remain only the bare upright posts. Here and there in the quarter are still a few patches of light—the façades of the hotels—in which groups still linger. Everywhere else is the heavy darkness from which emerge the twisted trunks of the old trees. It is late April. The rainy season is not far off. The rains have not yet come, but the heavy clouds drifting across the sky are their harbingers. It is six months since a drop of water has fallen. Everything is withered and dry, the pavements as well as the throats of human beings. It is more than dryness. It is desiccation. All things are bleached and polished as old bones. There is no water to wash the sidewalks. Mounds of garbage accumulate, pineapple rinds, scraps of bamboo, rotten oranges. When he shuts up shop, each stallkeeper neatly heaps up his little pile of rubbish. (The Chinese, despite his total lack of hygiene, is very clean.) As soon as he has swept his bit of sidewalk with his fan-shaped palm broom he—or she—lies down to sleep . . . at times on the rubbish heap, which serves as a pillow. Is this wisdom or resignation? The resignation of the Chinese is infinite. More than any other race, they are content with their lot. They seem to have no hatred. Is that what happiness is? . . .

I recall an old woman I used to see every day from my balcony. At 6 A.M. she would be at her post, sitting on a little bench behind a display case containing a few bamboo shoots and three dragon-apples. Every day and all day long she would sit there motionless until midnight. Never did she utter the slightest word. Was she a well of misery? In any case she was a well of silence. She would put out her arm to receive money, but no word ever issued from her mouth. What was she thinking about? Therein lies the mystery of China. Long after the street was deserted she would still be there. Finally she would stretch out on the spot like so many others and immediately appear to sink not into sleep but into nothingness.

When the Chinese is awake he is thoroughly alive and active, but once asleep he is corpselike. I have always been struck by the pained expression of most human beings when they are asleep. But in the Orient sleep is peculiarly tragic. Bodies do not have the look of abandon of people who are resting, but rather the rigidity of corpses. They have been annihilated, and their postures are deeply moving, as if they had suddenly been struck dead in the midst of a gesture. See that old man, completely inert, holding against his skeleton a little child; he is a petrified image of human tenderness. Look at that woman, still quite young, lying with her arms stretched toward her child, who lies sleeping five feet away (she suggests a corpse appealing to a living creature). At times the postures are grotesque, owing to the leanness of the limbs, the cavernous eyes, the gaping mouths with fleshless lips. Farther off is an entire family lying in a heap, the legs of some tossed over the bodies of others, pell-mell, as if a cataclysm had befallen them.

But most frightful of all are those who sleep with their eyes wide open. The eyes stare at you. They seem even to be following you as you go by.

Here and there something stirs in this cemetery of the living. A creature gets up with an air of infinite weariness and lies down again farther off. Another scratches himself. Another sits down at the curb. Though his figure is unclear in the darkness, I know what he is doing. He urinates—in China men take the squatting position—then resumes his pose.

I should add that it is not only the destitute who sleep

"*Rapid footsteps patter on the sidewalk, those of a prostitute . . . She glides along swiftly, thin and elegant in her form-fitting dress . . .*"

in the street. Opposite my hotel lives a jeweler. As it is too hot indoors (and the coming of the rainy season has made the heat humid), the family prefers to sleep in the open air, the wife on a camp bed, wrapped in a sheet that looks like a shroud, with her little girl beside her, and the husband simply stretched on a table in the middle of the pavement.

Rapid footsteps patter on the sidewalk, those of a prostitute. At three in the morning? Why not? Any hour is good. She glides along swiftly toward a definite goal, thin and elegant in her form-fitting dress, in striking contrast with the twisted corpses on the sidewalk. A rickshaw boy spies her, turns about, follows her hopefully. But she has already disappeared, swallowed up in the shadow of an alley. Perhaps that's where she lives. . . . The rickshaw boy moves off. For a moment longer can be heard the cracked clanging of his bell. Then, silence. All that remains is a living immobility, or a dead presence, there is no knowing which.

At dawn the bodies begin to squirm and get to their feet. Animation returns. Even before the sun is up the street vendors reassemble their displays. Already the porters, rhythmically bending under the weights of their loads, are trotting toward the market.

"At dawn, the bodies begin to squirm and get to their feet. Animation returns. Even before the sun is up, the street vendors reassemble their displays. Already the porters, rhythmically bending under the weight of their loads, are trotting towards the market."

XIX

BEFORE concluding, I should like to say a word about the Chinese of Cholon during the riots of March and April 1955 and about the sometimes odd aspects of their behavior.

On March 29, on the stroke of midnight, I was awakened from my sleep by explosions that were clearly not those of the firecrackers that the Sons of Heaven set off during their festivals in order to attract the attention of the gods.

I rushed to my balcony. There was a report of gunfire all along the road between Cholon and Saigon. It was the hour of night when the street was at its liveliest, with the Rainbow going in full swing, when idlers crowded the sidewalks, when the stalls of the food vendors were taken by assault and the pavement cooks were, so to speak, all in a stew. It was also the hour when the call girls made their way to one or the other hotel. All this bustle went on amidst a litter of greasy paper, bamboo rind, and rubbish of all kinds that strewed the pavement. It was then that the barking of heavy machine guns and the crackling of machine pistols burst forth.

Never had I seen so rapid a change. But the Chinese, more than any other people, have an animallike premonition of danger. Even before a danger is visible or audible the Chinese has already perceived it. How has he scented it? Exactly how does the approach of danger manifest itself? I do not know. In any case, primitives sense it, as do animals.

To be sure, there had been anxiety in the air in Cholon during the days preceding, but the shopkeeper that lurks in every Chinese had silenced this anxiety or had at least hidden it in order not to disturb business. The only visible sign had been something a bit furtive about their movements.

But that evening, hardly had the dry cough of the machine guns pierced the air than the aspect of Jaccareo Street was transformed. In less time than it takes to tell, the street stalls had folded up; the acetylene lamps had been extinguished; all was dark, so dark that it was as if a lid had been placed on the city. There was no longer a sound. Perhaps for the first time in its history Cholon had become totally silent. This instantaneous transition from bustle to absolute void was dumfounding.

All that could be heard was the mounting fire of the machine guns on the outskirts of town, and the whizzing of the tracer bullets. At the Sun Wah there was a deathlike stillness. I stood at my balcony with my ear cocked.

The firing lasted about forty-five minutes. Then it stopped completely. For the first time it would be possible to sleep soundly at the Sun Wah! But there was no question of sleeping. An overwhelming event had just begun. The balance of things had been violently upset. Two hours later the gunfire broke out again, then stopped with equal suddenness.

By the following morning Jaccareo Street had resumed its activity. But this was merely appearance, for actually everything had changed. Though the consequences of the upheaval were unforeseeable, one fact was clear: ten years after the riots that had followed the liberation, civil war had broken out anew. The Sects, with which the Diem government had reached a *modus vivendi* and to which it had accorded large sums of money to keep them quiet, were once again attacking.

I have no intention of going into the history of the affair. All I need do is indicate the strange situation prevailing in the country: lacking adequate resources, the government, in order to avoid engaging in a fratricidal war, had simply granted the Sects hostile to the regime (the Bin-Xuyen, Hoa-Hao, and Caodaists) the control of certain territories, including the city of Cholon. Furthermore, it had placed in the hands of the enemies—or rather, the "dissidents"—certain key posts, including the Public Security Office of Saigon itself, with the result that at the very seat of the government the police were in the hands of the enemies of the regime who, after remaining quiet for a while, had resumed hostilities without warning.

Exactly what had happened and how many persons had been killed during the shooting? I decided to go to Saigon to get information. But there were no rickshaws to be had. Their usual stand opposite the hotel was empty. The boys had taken flight.

243

I set out on foot. After walking for half an hour I managed to stop one. Despite his fears, I persuaded him to take me.

The boulevard linking the two cities was thronged. It was there that the enemy had attacked. House fronts had been riddled with bullets; pieces of wall had collapsed under mortar fire; tree trunks along the avenue had been slashed. The corpses had been removed, but here and there were pools of fresh blood.

In Saigon everything was topsy-turvy, though the town itself had not yet been damaged. People were running in all directions. That's what civil war is like. It has no front, it's everywhere. At one point it breaks out at ten o'clock; elsewhere at eleven. And those who run to the right to flee danger suddenly come up against machine guns and fall back in disorder to the left.

Sirens were wailing, jeeps were speeding like mad, going God knows where. Trucks rolled by, jammed with soldiers in battle array, all armed to the teeth with rifles, machine guns, pistols, and knives.

At the France-Asia Radio station, where I had friends, things were in complete upheaval. My friends were busily sorting photos of the night's events before sending them off. The sudden attack, they said, had been an act of blackmail aimed at getting more out of the government. In the Orient everything is a matter of bargaining. For a few thousand dollars a general passes over to the enemy camp with all his troops. For the time being, the two camps were dickering while the dead bodies were being collected. There was still a possibility of settling the matter.

I got back to Cholon with the little information I was

able to gather. All Cholon was on the alert. The Chinese were afraid of only one thing: that the war might spread to their town.

Nevertheless, I found a restaurant open and sat down at the terrace. After all, one has to eat.

I had barely started my meal when there was an explosion on the boulevard not far away. What followed was incredible. In a few seconds the street had emptied, everyone running to his lair with a speed more ratlike than human. I felt like a figure in a surrealist painting. There I was, seated at a table on the sidewalk, alone on a completely deserted street, with two hundred pairs of eyes staring at me through the iron shutters waiting to see what I would do.

I did not budge. Even at the risk of my life I had to show, if only once, my superiority, though I too wondered what was going to happen. But nothing happened. One by one the people emerged. Life went on as if there had been no break.

But the revolution was on its way. Though the machine guns remained silent for three days, everyone knew that things would not work out. At Cholon, life resumed its course, though people no longer strolled about. They slipped from house to house. The shopkeepers only half opened their iron curtains, ready to lower them at the slightest alert. Their instincts warned them that the worst was to come. I made an effort to reassure the people at my hotel that everything was going to be all right, but they shook their heads. "No, no. Very bad." The following day, things happened on Jaccareo Street. I had again insisted on being served outside, whereas everyone else now ate indoors, out of prudence, and at the far end of the dining room. All at once something broke. Though I had not heard a single shot, I saw the mob surge toward me, fleeing from the boulevard, this time not so much running as lifted by fear, lifted by the wind of the bullets. They must have told themselves that, however fast they ran, they could not outstrip the bullets. They threw themselves flat on the ground or flowed under tables that were outside. Their panic was so great that those who managed to get to their shops first pulled down their iron curtains, locking out their own families!

Was it a matter of cowardice? Not necessarily. As a soldier, the Chinese is just as brave as any other. But these people were not soldiers. Why should they get involved in the war? As Cholon was under the control of the Bin-Xuyen, the Chinese, realists that they were, had therefore paid the required sum so as to be left in peace. The Bin-Xuyen were supposed to protect them. The Chinese had counted on them. And now they were not respecting the agreement. The Chinese were furious, but what were they to do? Hurl themselves into the fighting? No, thank you. They were shopkeepers, peaceful folk. For nothing in the world would they have got mixed up in the brawl. Political events had perhaps gone beyond their local agreements. But they, the Chinese, did not want to get involved in the business. All they could do was lie low.

The affair had been going on for ten days, with lulls followed by fresh bursts of gunfire. That was what the fighting was like. There would be a violent surprise attack and then, before the enemy could reply, a rapid withdrawal. The quarter of Cholon where I lived had not yet been touched, but it would not be spared for

long. People lived half dug in, like rats. Indeed, there is
something ratlike about the Chinese. Not only are they
nibblers—they nibble all day long at hazelnuts and watermelon seeds—but there is something fleeting about them.
At the slightest sound they would slip with astonishing
agility through the cracks. With their amazing faculty of
adaptation they had in no time developed a technique of
flight and falling back. They would shut up shop as one
closes a box, burying their wares in some nearby nook.
The slightest crack was enough to conceal them. They
had become simply pairs of observing eyes, for their curiosity remained, despite their fear. They had to see what
was going on.

At the Sun Wah, too, everything had sunk into the
depths. As soon as there was the slightest disturbance outside, not a living soul was to be seen. I have already described the labyrinth of the Chinese hotel and the nooks
and corners it contains. It was in these crannies, in the
unending behind-the-scenes maze, that they took refuge.
The layout of the place was such that it would have saved
them, if ever the hotel were beset, from being trapped,
for the hotel had exits everywhere. In China everything
communicates; nothing is sharply delimited; nor is anything isolated. By means of stairways, corridors, and
open galleries the Sun Wah communicated with the
neighboring buildings to such a degree that there was no
telling where one began and the other ended.

It was only as a result of the events I have been describing that I discovered this fact. The first evening
when I returned late from Saigon, I was confronted with
a hermetically sealed door. The front of the building,
which was usually so open and cheery, had taken on, in

the light of the only lamppost in the square, a strangely forbidding look.

I rang but no one came. I was somewhat frightened, as the square in front of the hotel was particularly dangerous, owing to the fact that it offered access, by means of the bridge, to the other bank of the river, which was guarded by the enemy, who kept watch over the bridge day and night. At the entrance there were always shadows spying from behind the wall or one of the pillars of the bridge. Every shadow must have been holding in its hand or carrying in its pocket a revolver or a grenade. Two days earlier I had suddenly found myself keeping at a respectful distance from an individual of whom I could see in the darkness only his torn shirt and the gleaming barrel of a Luger. In other words, it was better not to linger in front of the hotel, and when, by chance, a rickshaw boy was willing to take me there, he was careful not to stop within range of the light and, as soon as he was paid, disappeared as fast as he could.

I had rung three times without getting an answer. There I stood, in the shadow of the square, with the uncomfortable feeling that there were eyes watching me. "Damn them," I said to myself, "they don't care a rap about my standing outside because they're scared!"

At last a shadow loomed behind the iron curtain. It was the night watchman, who made a sign to me to take the side street, which I did. There a wooden bar was drawn to open a way for me.

As for the circuit that I followed, I would be quite unable to retrace it. All I know is that there were bodies everywhere, lying three-quarters naked on the steps of the stairways, heaped against each other. But in front there was no one. The floor corridor, where people usually strolled up and down as if it were a street, was deserted. So was the lobby, formerly the public square. How many nights was I to spend that way, watching from my balcony, with the weird impression of being the only survivor of what had hitherto been a busy caravanserai. I mean at night, for during the day life went on, though subdued, behind the façade, which remained stubbornly closed. Whatever happens, the Chinese needs to function. Though the Rainbow had closed, putting its taxi girls out of work, the prostitutes continued their functions. And I could still hear laughter from the rear of the establishment, which proved that the Chinese were still amusing themselves, though perhaps they were laughing in order not to hear what was going on outside. I could also hear in various compartments the shuffling of mahjong tiles.

My first reaction was that there was something shocking about all this. But the Chinese cannot be alone; they must communicate, particularly during a time of crisis. They were unable to understand my remaining stubbornly alone at the outpost, as it were, of the hotel. Every now and then one of the boys would slip up to my room, tug at my sleeve, and say, "Here very bad. Come this way." They could not understand my being so serious. Despite the fact that they were frightened, far more frightened than I, they had to distract themselves with joking and laughter.

As for Chinese humor, I witnessed an odd demonstration of it one morning.

All of the preceding day there had been bombings on the outskirts of Cholon. It was no longer a matter only of machine-gun fire, for heavy mortar and cannons had been brought into play. At night, fires, which had evidently been lit by criminal hands, had ravaged the right bank of the river directly in front of my window. Never had I seen such a spectacle. Not only did the fire, which had been set at exactly the same moment at three different points, bar the entire horizon with a curtain of dancing flames, not only did the crackling of the bamboo supports of the straw huts which was audible miles away make the catastrophe more striking, for the roar of the fire was even more fearful than the sight of it, but the heat of the mass blazing away behind the black line of the warehouses along the river had caused a gigantic whirl of air that drew the flames upward to a height of three hundred feet. The result of this was an enormous blast that I could feel against my cheek, and it was this blast that had driven people beyond the zone of fire, just as it had bowed the branches of the trees and knocked down doors with the violence of its pressure. About thirty thousand people had thus been "blasted" toward the river in a darkness that, outside the zone of fire, was opaque, owing to the fact that the electric cables had been cut.

When they reached the Arroyo they dared not cross and simply remained there cowering, waiting for day to break. At the first gleams of dawn, when all that remained of their bank was a heap of ruins, they rushed to the bridge with the feverish movements and panicky expressions of frightened animals that are displayed by fugitives everywhere, crowding onto the narrow passage like cattle driven from behind, colliding with each other like creatures half out of their minds, without control over their movements. Shoulders would thrust forward, but the rest of the body would not follow. Their arms flayed in the air. The loads they were carrying kept dropping from their hands and when they attempted to pick them up they lost their balance under the pressure of the mob. From the charred landscape across the bridge surged an endless tide of human beings, fleeing the land as rats flee a sinking ship. The bridge was so loaded that it seemed to sink beneath the weight. All fellow feeling had disappeared. It was every man for himself. Anyone who fell was immediately trampled. Human beings seemed stripped to their essentials, in the grip of utter fear. The spectacle was not only incoherent but grotesque.

At that point the people of the Sun Wah emerged from their lairs, probably having been assured by one of their number that there was no further danger. There they stood, watching the scene from the top of the terrace, missing not a bit of the spectacle. They were watching the others flee, each carrying with him his most precious possession, like Frenchmen during the exodus of 1940, one man with a scrawny dog, another with a canary in a cage.

One of them was pushing his cow. Of all that milling mob, the cow was the only calm creature. No doubt it thought it was being led to pasture as usual. But pasturing on a bridge! The cow hesitated, resisting the onward thrust of the mob. It reached the steps, stopped, and sniffed. Its instinct told it that there was nothing in front. And the crowd was stopped by the cow, which had planted itself crosswise in self-defense and was blocking the entire passage . . . until, under the human drive forward, it was hustled along. It stumbled down the steps and fell to its knees. Before it had time to get up the crowd flowed over its body and into the square.

A group of thirty rickshaw boys were standing by, for they realized that this was a windfall for them. But what were thirty vehicles of this kind for such a human mass! Each was being solicited by twenty arms at once. And, as in any exodus, everyone was trying to outbid everyone else. "I'll give you a bag of rice! . . . I'll give you my daughter!" The fare from Cholon to Saigon, which normally was fifteen piastres, rose to a thousand!

The rickshaws were taken by assault, loaded pell-mell with human beings and bundles. Then off they went.

The rest of the crowd stood bewildered. But when the fugitives got to the other side they no longer knew where to turn. They knew *what* they were fleeing but not *where* to flee. They hesitated, put down their bundles. The autos whizzing by made them back up toward the steps, only to be pushed forward again. We were witnessing an ebb and flow of uncertainty and anguish. And their fear was all the more absurd in that there was no longer any danger. But the fear subsisted.

The entire hotel had now come out to the terrace of the Sun Wah, the manager, the boys, the clients, and even the prostitutes, who had remained overnight out of fear. Some of the men were wearing only a pair of shorts; others were in silk pajamas. The purple or pale pink pajamas of the prostitutes added an incongruous note. Everyone was writhing with laughter. Their loud guffaws, their sarcasm in the face of this ghastly exodus against a background of charred ruins, the burnt odor of which filled

"The prostitutes in their purple or pale pink pajamas . . ."

our nostrils, were bewildering. The sight of those yellow faces, suddenly so cruel and snickering after having displayed such fear, the sight of these spectators pointing at one or another unhappy creature trammeled in his fear and turning round and round like an animal at bay, was staggering. At first I was seized with indignation, almost with anger, at such a demonstration, for the laughter had the repulsive, not to say ignoble, quality of the attitude of spectators who, from the tiers, snicker as they watch a victim thrashing about in the middle of an arena.

But it was not really that. The truth is that the Chinese has such a passion for spectacles that he cannot restrain himself. And even if it is he himself whom the tragedy is befalling, the comic note that accompanies all tragedy does not escape him. And if the comic element strikes him more forcibly than the tragic, he will laugh, because, like all men close to nature, he is sensitive to natural forces, and what can be more in the order of nature than the mingling of the comic and tragic? There is nothing morbid in such behavior, as one might be tempted to believe. Quite the contrary, it is eminently healthy. It is akin to the advice that a German friend gave me one day when I was feeling utterly miserable. "Eat!" she said. "When a person is unhappy, he should eat." The idea of sitting down at the table to calm my wretchedness had, for the moment, seemed to me thoroughly monstrous. But before I knew it she had taken a tin of pâté de foie gras and some sauerwurst and made me swallow the food with shots of the white brandy which, she said, "dissolves sorrow." And before long we were both in high spirits, I more so than she, because laughter is a defense of the human organism.

I have seen Russians laugh after relating the murder of a member of their family during the Revolution. They did so only to repress the grief that was rising into their throats. In like manner, I once heard a Spanish woman —she too was close to nature—describe to me, with many comic details, the burial of her father, who, nevertheless, had been dearer to her than anyone in the world, because she had needed, at a certain point, a safety valve for her sorrow and this safety valve had been offered her by the ill-fitting formal jacket of her brother, who was chief mourner. "He was so terribly funny! He looked like a wet hen with his tails dragging behind!" Thus, if a man has a certain element of simplicity in him, he can move quite naturally from tears to laughter, and probably the Chinese indifference, shocking though it may seem, is merely a simple view of things on the part of the man for whom death, too, is a spectacle.

Thus I had seen the people of the Sun Wah pass without transition from panic to unbounded hilarity and, a few hours later, back to panic. The battle was now reaching their quarter. Not only were tracer bullets whizzing everywhere like hornets, but heavy mortars were ripping the ground. Along the river the boatmen were frantically pushing their barges beyond the orbit of the projectiles. This time it was impossible for anything to go on functioning in Cholon. Even though the Chinese suffered only accidental deaths—for what was going on was a massacre among the Vietnamese—life for them there was no longer possible. The upheaval of Indo-China had only just begun. The French, who had been kept there by business, were beginning to leave the country. When they were gone there would be a vacuum, a vacuum that would not be filled by Mr. Diem's Vietnamese, who were quite incapable of filling it. It would be filled by the Viets of the north, the Communists, and also, no doubt, in the commercial sphere, by the Japanese, who were waiting impatiently for the moment when they could enter the country with their cheap goods.

In short, the Chinese realized that their time in Indo-China was up. But where were they to go? It was out of the question to return to China, at least as long as it was not possible to understand clearly what was going on there. Indonesia had just been closed to them as the result of an agreement contracted at Bandung by Chou En-lai. There remained the bordering countries, Cambodia and Thailand. But these were already swarming with Chinese and the frightened governments of those countries were closing their frontiers. The rich Chinese had, nevertheless, managed to get through, but not the great mass. And these 600,000 human beings, most of them little people whose ancestors had fled from China a century and a half before to establish themselves in Cholon and to build a progressive city, had to prepare themselves once again for an exodus, without knowing where they could go on living.